To Irene,

with

And   ings.

From Joan.
xxx

When the Christmas candles are burned
out;
The carols have died away;
the star is set;
All the radiant song-filled night is past
thou alone, the Eternal, remainest, and
thou art enough.
Remain in me, more beautiful,
more beloved,
more real than any of the romance
that clusters around Thy birthday.

SAFETY LAST

BOOKS BY THE SAME AUTHOR

REFLECTIONS

'SAFETY LAST!'

Stirring Tales of the Pacific

BY

RITA F. SNOWDEN

*Once I thought to find on earth
Love, perfect and complete,
Now I know it carries wounds
In its hands and feet.*

THE EPWORTH PRESS

(EDGAR C. BARTON)

25–35 City Road, London, E.C.1

For my friend
'Lena H.

Contents

List of Illustrations

Introduction

WHEN I would essay some impossible task in youth, one loved and trusted would say to me: ' You can't put the ocean into a bucket.' I know that now; but this is my attempt to put some part of the world's greatest ocean into a book. Fitchett assures us that this romantic, dangerous Pacific exceeds in area all the dry land in the world. Here, too, one might pour in—had one the magic power—every drop of three Atlantics, or if one chose, seventy Mediterraneans.

Romance, danger, and beauty are here. Tradition, too, though men count the Pacific new, and speak of her lands with their faces to the future. The people of Tonga have preserved the names of their sovereigns back a thousand years—the present sovereign tracing her descent from ancient chiefs who ruled the Tongans before the Normans conquered England.

In this Pacific of stirring tales are tens of thousands of islands, ranging in size from the world's largest, New Guinea, and Borneo, down to mere dots of palm-covered coral. And here it is difficult to know which has been worse, the ferocity of the brown man, or the devilry of the white man, aided by his muskets and barter.

It is not surprising if our approach to the Pacific be coloured by those dreams of youth when we lay in the long grass reading *Kidnapped* and *Treasure Island*. The ghosts of Long John Silver and his crew have roved the Pacific ever since. We might, any minute, raise hands to eyes to catch sight of a black vessel flying the Jolly Roger, the Black Flag, or more sinister, no flag at all.

The Spaniards came first into these waters—discovering

much, claiming much, and keeping nothing. Balbao was Spain's claimant—the first white man to set eyes on this mighty ocean, and claim it entire, seen and unseen, in the name of the King of Castile and Leon.

The Dutch came next, and left behind them a fine record. Abel Jansen Tasman was their man—discoverer of New Zealand and Tonga and Fiji.

The French came—and though much of their way was marked with tragedy—they sprinkled a few French names about the Pacific.

England's man—Captain Cook—proved himself the chief figure, his voyages unsurpassed in sea history for skill, daring, and endurance.

Yet, the lasting pattern of the Pacific's life owes its shape to none of these. It has been, and is still, the men and women of Christian spirit who have accomplished most. In some parts a few years have witnessed such startling and dramatic changes that the story reads like a postscript to the Acts of the Apostles. So real and so widespread has been the missionary spirit that more brown men than white men have given their lives for their fellows in the Pacific.

Great names of white leaders leap to the memory. I will not be tempted to list them all—Williams, Chalmers, Paton, Marsden, Leigh, Selwyn, Patteson—their story is enshrined in the annals of the South Seas.

I have set myself here, rather to tell stirring tales that I have heard from those who have sought *safety last* in this great field. Many of these have not been written down before. Tracking down clues has meant for me a correspondence reaching to many parts of the world, and contacts with many living dangerously in these terrible, stirring days.

I have followed no order in setting down these tales—time, place, colour, denomination—these things matter less and less. Only the things of the spirit matter—courage, faith, loyalty, love. So here an American airman rubs shoulders with a member of the British Empire, and an islander from the battle-scarred Solomons with a German priest in the jungle.

The Pacific has always been the scene of great change. Widely held amongst scientists is the theory that important land masses and large populations have disappeared in this area in past ages, as the result of volcanic action and great subsidences. It is believed that these cataclysms have engulfed whole civilizations—that empires have sunk into the sea and left scarcely a trace.

The fury of war has scarred the Pacific. Changes of another character are at hand. The Cross has been upheld here in the colourful past, nor will there be lacking those with the will and the wherewithal to do it in the new days. The people are not perfect—but one thing is true, the conquests of the spirit are not a past story.

Here is my 'bucketful'—not the whole ocean, but a little bucketful of pure water.

R. F. S.

One

'Loyalty Lives Still'

How can one retell the story of Vuza's heroism and loyalty that brave men have called a story beyond words?

What manner of man is Vuza? The answer is a Solomon Island policeman. A Christian, married to a girl trained by the South Sea Evangelical Mission. It was Vuza who introduced Christian things into his own village. Vuza stands six feet high, his soft, bronze, gleaming hair standing straight up in an impressive Solomon Island *coiffure*. His splendid physical strength is covered by a natural grace of movement, his forehead is broad and good. There is something unforgettably attractive about him. He has an inward serenity.

When suddenly war came to the Solomons, and Japanese bombs blasted the villages of the people, Vuza was troubled. He did not like the coming of the Japanese. He had seen them spying their way through the islands for years; he knew the boasts of one who had worked at Tulagi as a carpenter, ostensibly, while he carried out his underground task. And now that they had come, he didn't know what was going to happen next.

What Vuza did in those first months after the landing, nobody knows. All we know is that when the Americans arrived to help drive back the invaders, Vuza was there at once to help them with all that he had to give.

The tracks in the jungle were well known to him. And where the Japanese were he soon knew. Alone, he set out to gather information.

Then somehow, we don't know how, he fell into enemy hands. He saw that he was trapped. They asked him questions —wanted to know where the Americans were. One of their

12

number, the little ex-carpenter of Tulagi, recognized him, but Vuza would not utter a word. They offered him bribes, but he would not speak.

Then exasperated, they dropped their promises and bribes and commenced to threaten. They tied him to a tree in a clearing in the jungle. It looked as though they had finished with him. They left him, but after a little while they came back. This time they had exchanged bribes for bayonets. Vuza saw the bayonets —he couldn't help but see them, and he knew what they meant. Still, in the deep places of his heart he *knew* what loyalty meant. That he knew it well was proven in the next few hours in that little open space in the jungle.

There, tied, far from his friends, Vuza was given one last chance. Would he take it? When, to their chagrin, those who had put him there saw that he meant to keep his lips sealed, they drove a bayonet through his arm. He winced, strained at the thongs that bound him, still he did not speak. Moments passed. Then came a second bayonet thrust— this time through the neck. The Japanese officer in charge shouted his last command. Patience was at an end. One of his men came forward, at his word, and drove his bayonet to the hilt through Vuza's body. He had not spoken one word.

Reckoning him as dead, they went away, leaving him tied to the tree in the jungle.

But Vuza did not die. His strength was ebbing, but somehow, as night fell, he contrived to chew through the thongs and get himself free.

The American line was a long way off—twenty miles—but Vuza made up his mind that he would at least try for it. He had information that must be given. Propping himself against a nearby tree trunk, he waited a moment. Then he started off. Crawling, walking, staggering—every few hundred yards he rested. It was agony, but he pushed on—on and on through the jungle, on and on through the hours of the night, until an American sentry heard something stirring. He snapped out his challenge. Was it enemy or friend? Then out of the darkness came Vuza, crawling on his hands and knees.

His strength, they saw, was almost gone. He must be got to a doctor, they said. But Vuza said, 'No, no, take me first to an officer. The doctor can wait. I must tell what I know.'

They heard his amazing story. Then they handed him over to the tenderness and skill of the doctor.

Days passed, weary days. At last there came a day unique in the long history of the Islands. On that day, which brave men talk of still, Vuza the Solomon Islander received the George Medal, and the American Silver Star. And those who knew his story knew that these two honours—never lightly bestowed—had never been more splendidly given than to this son of the Islands who had given a new content to the word loyalty.

Two

The One-eyed God-maker

A TIMID knock at the door.

'Come in!' Mr. Goldie called, without looking up from his work. He was just settling down to his translation work, and didn't want to be disturbed.

It was seven o'clock on Monday morning. The life of the head mission station had already begun. First *lotu*, or morning prayers, then work—work on the plantation, work on the boats, in the carpenter's shop, preparation for school for a couple of hours later—a hundred and one things.

Again came the knock at the study door, and in answer to the second invitation to 'come in!' some one fumbled at the door-knob. It was evident to the missionary that some native un-accustomed to doors of any kind, some one from a distance, probably, was seeking him. While he wondered, the door responded to fumbling and he turned to meet the visitor as it opened.

It was Bela Bangara, the one-eyed god-maker of Roviana, whose home was a village about ten miles away. His trade had once been a profitable one, for he was a wonderful carver, and had carved most of the idols which the people worshipped. Like one of old time, he had found lately that his craft had become endangered through the spread of the Gospel. So he had bitterly opposed it.

Now, however, as he stood silent before the missionary, the crafty, cruel old idol-maker seemed changed. What had happened to him? The shifty look, the hideous grin had gone. A tender, soft expression illumined his face.

The missionary saw, and understood. A great joy filled his heart.

'Thank God, Bela Bangara,' he said.

'Yes, thank God, sir.'

'Sit down and tell me all about it.' And the old man sat down on the floor of the study.

'It was yesterday,' he said. 'I listened to the preaching. The preacher told us about the blind man who sat begging by the wayside—the Saviour passing by. Sir, I am that blind beggar.

'Then I went back to my house, and on my mat lay thinking of what I had heard. My little boy came in, and throwing himself on his mat, began to read some words from the Holy Book which you have just translated into our language. He read:

'"The gods are the work of man's hands. They have mouths, but they speak not, eyes have they, but they see not: they have ears but they hear not: noses have they, but they smell not: they have hands, but they handle not."

'I thought of my own gods. As I lay with my eyes shut, the idols which I had fashioned seemed to pass one by one before me—Mungeri, the fishing god, Lingomo, the fighting god—blind, deaf, and dumb, every one of them.

'The ears which I myself had fashioned were deaf to my cry; the lips which my own hands had made were dumb—they could not frame an answer to my prayer: they had hands but no power to help me.

'I listened as my boy read on. He read: "They that make them are like unto them: so is every one that trusteth in them."

'Yes, sir,' he went on, 'like unto them—blind, deaf, dumb, helpless. Oh, a great longing filled my soul. A cry went up from me to the Christ, "Lord, that I might receive my sight".

'Then my boy turned over the pages and read again, and it seemed, as he read, as if a voice was speaking to me, "The Lord is my Light and my Salvation. . . . The Lord is the Strength of my life, of whom shall I be afraid."

MAORI GREETS PAKEHA

[see page 32]

'"O Lord," I cried, "be *my* light—touch the eyes of my blind heart, and give *me* sight."

'I must have spoken aloud, for my lad, putting aside the Book, knelt and joined his simple prayer to mine. As we prayed it seemed as if a covering fell from my eyes. I saw and understood, and a great peace filled my heart. I said, "Let us rise early in the morning, and go to the Mission and ask Mr. Goldie about this."

'So I have come to tell you these things. Tell me, can Christ really save me? Can He save Bela Bangara?'

Together the idol-maker and the missionary knelt in the quiet study, and He who alone can change the heart and transform the life of an old savage, came into the heart of old Bela Bangara that day, assuring him of pardon, giving him light and understanding, and filling his soul with peace.

As they rose from their knees, and took each other's hands to say good-bye, the old man said, 'I am sorry to interrupt you in your work, sir'.

At that the heart of the missionary was very full.

'*God send me many such interruptions, Bela Bangara,*' was the reply.

B

Three

The Brown Madonna

We bring our varying gifts to Thee,
And Thou rejectest none.

H E was an artist, a master craftsman, that little old fellow
with the hard-chiselled face, blue-scrolled with tattoo lines,
and the hunched shoulders that came of a tumble in his babyhood, when a careless sister let him slip from her shawl. Hunch-
back, but no cripple, as you would have seen had you been by
when the Arawa Constabulary fell in for a fighting expedition
into the ranges. Short but not squat, rifle in hand, tomahawk in
belt, a seventy-pound swag on his bent but powerful shoulders,
short-kilted, Patoromu[1] looked a perfectly competent warrior.
You would have noticed also that Patoromu, though the smallest
man in the Maori company, carried the biggest load of them all.
On top of his *pikau* of rations, cartridges and blanket, was made
fast a bulky parcel wrapped up in a bit of flax mat.

Patoromu was an artist before he became a Government
guerrilla soldier. Fighting or no fighting, he would not be
parted from that *pikau*. If you watched him unroll the mat, you
would have seen a block of totara wood, half-hollowed out in
the shape of an oval bowl, and in it, carefully wrapped again,
some chisels of various sizes, a gouge and a club-shaped whale-
bone mallet. These were his carving tools; the block of totara
was his raw material which presently would take shape under his
fingers, cunningly incised in graceful and sometimes fantastic
native designs.

Patoromu's life work was the carving of shapeless wood into

[1] The name is the Maorified form of the Bible name Bartholomew.

things of beauty. In camp, when his comrades were lying wrapped in their blankets, comfortably smoking and dreaming after the day's march, he would be at work by one of the fires, tapping with mallet and chisel, advancing his heart's design a little further.

Once, in a bush skirmish, a *Hauhau* bullet plunked into one of his half-carved *watuhuius*. The Arawa dashed into the twilight depths of the mountain-side, and shot some of those rebels.

Later, in bivouac, Patoromu said his prayers and told his beads, for he was a pious son of the Church, and led the services in the contingent's base camp.

So many years passed. At last the guerrilla wars were over, the Arawa Constabulary were disbanded, and Patoromu carved in peace in his lakeside home. He made model canoes, he carved paddles, pipes, spade handles, palisade posts, and wall slabs, even the face of mankind, for he was a tattooer as well as a woodworker. A serene picture the old fellow made, squatting there absorbed in his art.

The new church was going up at Ruapeka Bay, below the carved palisades of the *pa*. It was the church of Patoromu's adopted faith. The Arawa people, down to the children, were hard at work on the interior. Outside it might look European, that pretty church; inside it was truly Maori, with carvings and painted rafters scrolled in the form of waves, fern fronds and bush flowers; with graceful *arapaki* panelling, and ecclesiastical emblems worked in laths and flax and bush-vine. Every scroll, bright-painted rafter, every stitch of wall-weaving, was a labour of love.

'Now, Patoromu,' queried the good Father one day, 'What are you going to do for our new church? You haven't forgotten, have you?'

'No, Father,' answered the carver, 'I have not forgotten. I shall make a gift to the beautiful church; it shall be the best carving I have ever done. I have been working at it for a long time. Wait, and you shall see.'

In the early morning of the very day on which the new church was to be opened and consecrated, Patoromu, the little wood-carver, presented himself with a bulky mat-enveloped package in his arms, a burden almost as big as himself. He lowered it carefully and drew off the mats. There lay revealed his masterpiece. The little man trembled with suppressed excitement and pride. His eyes glistened as he held the triumph of his art for the Father's admiration. Lovingly and reverently he handled it; anxiously he regarded the priest's face.

'It is to place on the altar shrine," he said.

The good Father's expression was a study in mixed emotions. He saw before him a carving of the Madonna with the Infant in her arms. Patoromu had done the best that was in him. The mother was admirable, considered as a Maori mother—tattooed of lips and chin, she gazed out into space with a proud Maori *rangatira*[1] expression. Her hair was done in the Maori manner, with three proud *huia* feathers, a greenstone pendant hung from one ear, her form scrolled and spiralled in intricate patterns of delicate grace. She held her Child athwart her breast.

The kindly priest stood long in silence. He hated to wound feelings; he discerned the artist soul, the devotion behind the gift. But he shook his head.

'It is beautiful, my son,' he said. 'But—remember the Bishop might not admire it as I do when he comes to us. Indeed, it would be so strange to him. He would say this and that, and I might be sent from the Arawa people, whom I love. No, Patoromu, it grieves me to say it, but you must take the carving away. Wrap it up again before any other sees it.'

Without a word, the little wood-carver, dazed with the shock of rejection, rolled up his masterpiece in its mats, and bore it away.

〇〉   〇〉   〇〉

Hours later, that day, when the church bell was ringing for the opening of the new church, sudden cries were heard coming

[1] Rangatira—chief.

from the open space between the meeting house and the pumice-beached bay. The few idle folk, enjoying their soak in the warm springs, gaped with amazement. It was Patoromu, the little wood-carver, apparently gone crazy. Stripped, he was dancing a furious dance in the middle of the open space, gripping his long-handled tomahawk; he leapt like a wild goat; he uttered a fearful cry. As they watched, he stopped with a final thud; then he paced up and down, up and down. Yes, it had been too much for his mind; he had gone crazy.

And he lived on with his poor, distracted mind.

But with all his Tewera practice the old wood-carver secretly cherished his Madonna. Wrapped in fine native mats she stood in a corner of his *whare*[1] all his days. When he lay dying, a European friend sat by his side, and with almost his last breath, Patoromu bade his friend take the church-banned gift. *Some day it will be given public recognition. When that day comes, those who see it—knowing the true story of its making—will surely discern in it the beautiful offering of a true heart.*

[1] A Maori house.

Four

One More Flame!

THE young Chinese Governor of the island was puzzled. His people on the levels tended camphor plantations, but away up in the mountains of Formosa they were wild and savage, and in days gone by were wilder still.

Through the dense forests and jungles, Gohu came to his people. They had been head-hunters for generations, and for as long as any could remember, had offered human sacrifices to the gods.

Gohu gathered them around him. 'My people,' he said, 'prosperity will never come to you whilst you live in fear of each other; your little children will never learn to laugh and play till the horrors of your cruelty are gone, and they can go to their sleep without fear.

꧁   ꧂   ꧃

For years Gohu could do very little, but by degrees they learned that his ways were good ways, and a period of comparative peace settled upon them.

Then came a dreadful season of drought. The oldest amongst them had not witnessed anything like it; the ground began to crack beneath their feet; their crops withered, the very streams themselves dried up. The people were parched. Famine and death stared them in the face. Then one day, the priests of the people came to Gohu, their governor.

'The gods are angry with us,' they said, 'we must offer sacrifice! Then the rain will surely come.'

Gohu said, 'No, my people! It is an order. There shall be no sacrifice!'

But the people were maddened by thirst and hunger. Again they came; and again he sent them away.

'Give us only one—one who does not matter—a child!' they cried, 'even a child will do! But we must sacrifice! Give us some one who doesn't matter much!'

Then the priests, because they knew no other, in their blind anxiety went among the people and stirred them up to rebellion. They came to Gohu's house and clamoured wildly at his door. Gohu's heart was sad, for he loved his people. At last he said, 'Well, let it be. To-morrow morning, get you up very early before the rising of the sun. Go up to the sacred grove and let the priests build the altar and kindle the flame upon it, and there will come out to you a man clothed in a red robe from head to foot, with a red hood over his head and down on to his shoulders. Let your priests at once strike him, and offer him up as a sacrifice. It is a promise.'

Pacified, the people returned to their homes. Very early in the morning, before the rising of the sun, they gathered in the sacred grove. The fire was kindled on the altar, and just as the sun rose, even as Gohu had said, there came out to them a man clothed in a red robe, having also a red hood. There was a hush, the priest stood ready. The knife, upraised, struck deep and true. For a moment of time the figure swayed—the people held their breath. Then a paralysing cry went up from the people, for as the figure fell, the hood dropped back, and the face they saw was the face of Gohu.

Never would they forget it!

Years have passed since that morning hour when the wild people of the mountains of Formosa offered up their last human sacrifice, but if you go there to-day, the descendants of those same people will take you quietly and directly up a winding track to a simple grave among the hills, and there, carved in solid rock you will read beneath the name of Gohu, these beautiful words:

A CANDLE
THAT IN GIVING LIGHT TO OTHERS,
CONSUMED ITSELF.

Five

The Old Pilot Hands Over

THE white man and the old pilot, Gumi, drifted through the Manning Straits. The old fellow was in reminiscent mood. He was one of the high chiefs of New Georgia, and had been one of the most notorious head-hunters.

'Do you see that little island away over there on the starboard side, sir?' asked the old fellow, and his hand followed the direction of his eyes.

'Yes, what about it?'

'We had a great fight there one day, a very great fight.'

'Tell me about it, Gumi. Did you fall out and fight amongst yourselves, or was it with the people of Lauru, or the people of Sambana?'

'No,' said the old man, 'it was not our own people. We came over on a turtle-hunting expedition, and found the Lauru men poaching on our hunting ground. They thought we were not aware of their presence, and hoped by hiding to take us by surprise, or else to make good their escape in the darkness of night. We let them believe that we did not know of their whereabouts, but we laid our plans.' The old man paused a moment. 'Just before dawn we fell upon them. They fought well, but'—and the old man spat in disgust—'the Lauru men could never stand before the Roviana men.'

'Were many killed, Gumi?'

'They were all killed. Some only wounded, jumped into the water, and the current, strong there, carried them away; but we took two hundred heads back with us to Roviana that day. Ah, it was a great day!' The fires of reminiscence kindled the old pilot's eyes.

It is true, well-nigh unbelievable things can happen with the passing of the years. As the white man, Missionary Goldie, sat recalling that day in the Manning Straits, the old chief's son sat at his elbow typing out the translation of Mark's Gospel. Leaning over his shoulder he was not a little moved to read in Sunga's native language: '*All things are possible to him that believeth*'

Sunga was a Christian youth, clean of body and mind, with light and liberty in his every movement. At first his old father had bitterly opposed his having anything to do with a new way of life. But with a clear determination, Sunga had come to the parting of the ways. Addressing his father, with due consideration, he said: 'I have become a Christian, and I want to be received into the Christian Church. If you give your consent, then all will be well between us: I will try to consider your wishes as my father, in the future as I have always done. But——' after a pause, 'if you refuse, then I must make my own decision.' Sunga had become Christ's man!

Many years passed, then there came into his life an hour of unspeakable happiness. That morning, in the presence of his friends, Sunga led his old father, Gumi, of more than one famous head-hunting raid, up to the front of the Church for Christian baptism. He was the only candidate that morning, but what joy!

As the pioneer missionary, Goldie, beheld this miracle, his mind flashed back to those words that years before he had read over the shoulder of the old pilot's son: '*All things are possible to him that believeth.*'

Six

'As the Generations Pass'

THE little Maori *pa*[1] snuggled amongst the hills; so quiet was its life, that many in the country town but two miles away, hardly remembered that it was there.

In the long ago days when Tawhiao was Maori king, two young brothers had quarrelled, and one of them had come to this lonely spot to make a home for his people.

Only a thin thread of a track winding up beside a railway line led to the *pa*, which lay concealed by a maze of fern and *tea-tree*.[2] Kauia's people in this remote spot among the hills, treasured the belief that their site was sacred because the King and his party had once travelled their way, camping for the night. Some said that the name of the little *pa* had actually been chosen by the King; certainly its name signified that it was established by a youth of the ancient line of chiefs.

So Kauia gathered his people about him; he built them a sacred meeting house where the problems of their simple life could be shared, their arts and crafts practised, and the precious legends handed down. A second meeting house was built in after years, to serve the more playful side of their lives—their games and *hakas*,[3] and their interest in the European customs. Kauia loved to have his people happy.

For years the Christianity of the white people touched the *pa* but little. Off and on, when attending Maori gatherings in other parts, where Christian services were conducted, Kauia would listen. Like many others of his tribe, he was an adherent of a Maori religion, Hauhauism. The years passed.

Then one day there came to the little *pa*, a Sister of the his-

---

[1] Maori settlement. [2] Native shrub. [3] A spirited dance.

toric Methodist Church. Kauia listened intently to the Gospel
story that she brought.

Again and again, on her journeyings, she came, leaving always
with Kauia's warm invitation to come again. Time went by, and
as old Kauia continued to listen, and to ponder over what he
heard, his heart was strangely moved, and he became Christian.

When the Sister came again, plans were made for a Sunday
school for the little ones. In her many journeyings, the Sister
soon found two young women ready to help with this work.
They, too, loved the great Maori people.

The little Sunday school was a great success; from the start,
its members gathered in Kauia's small meeting house—babies,
bigger boys and girls, fathers and mothers, and even grand-
parents! How those children sang! How their faces shone!

Though old Kauia did not always attend, the young teachers
never left without visiting him and his wife in their simple *whare*
home. Unlike the children of the *pa*, old Kauia had never
mastered English, and the purport of every story had to reach
him through an interpreter.

What a happy day it was when regular preaching services
were begun by the visiting Maori ministers.

Soon a bigger company than usual gathered, the aged Kauia
and his wife were both present. During the worship the old man
rose to speak. Silence awhile, and then with dignity he began:
'Until you people of the Methodist Mission came with the Gospel, the *pakeha*[1] hardly knew that the *pa* was here. No one
visited us and no one cared for our welfare. Then you were sent
with the Gospel, and the Gospel has made all different. Now you
and your *pakeha* friends come to the *pa*[2] to visit us.' After a
moment's pause, the old chief moved on to the climax of his
oration. He told his people how that he would not be much
longer with them. 'Whilst I have been with you,' he continued,

[1] European.
[2] The name of the *pa* is Whakaaratamaiti. King Tawhiao—the
Maori king who figures on our New Zealand pound notes.

'I have gone round when the sacred time has come, telling you to gather for worship. Soon my tongue will call you no longer; I shall have gone; but before that time, it is my wish to have a bell. I shall be silent, but its tongue shall call you to worship.'

With characteristic Maori graciousness, the old man turned then to thank those whom God had sent to them with the Gospel. The pioneer Sister[1] and the two young teachers would never forget the old man's closing words: 'Before all was darkness, now all is light!'

Soon the teachers and the Sister had gathered together enough to buy a bell. The old man was pleased; and the great day came when it was hung in a worthy place at the entrance of the large meeting house.

Whilst old Kauia was with his people, he expressed a wish that his daughter should become the guardian of the bell, that its voice should never be silenced.

Early in the winter of nineteen-thirty-four, Chief Kauia Tapuke passed from his people—an aged man of a hundred-and-twelve. *But his Christian witness continues to-day, the simple melodious notes of his bell, ringing out over the homes, calling his people to Christian worship.*

[1] The Sister of the Methodist Church—Sister Nicholls.

Seven

'Greater Love . . .'

Y ou would know the little island of Sohana because it stands high, its precipitous cliffs skirted by a coral ledge past which the deep waters of the Buka passage swirl with amazing swiftness.

It was a typical outpost of Empire, where the Australian Ensign was proudly raised each morning at sunrise, and lowered each evening at sunset. Sohana was headquarters of the Government officer, and native chiefs were summoned here to learn the will of the Government. From time to time medical orderlies came, one from each village to procure the medicines that the Government provided. Here was administered for the benefit of all, the white man's justice. Here, too, would foregather each steamer-time, as many as ten or a dozen white men from the plantations scattered along a hundred and fifty miles of coastline, men who, more often than not, had seen no other white man since last steamer-time six or seven weeks earlier. So the little island of Sohana meant much to the people living in those parts.

Then, almost overnight everything was changed. In the place of the Australian Ensign, the Rising Sun floated aloft in the breeze. Where once had been peaceful green lawns now bristled anti-aircraft guns. Where had been orderliness, was now a fury of building, as the materials from wrecked plantation and mission buildings were assembled.

The arrogant newcomers thought still to summon the native chiefs to Sohana, but, alas, Sohana of peace-time had gone. Those who came in answer to the summons now, of course, came to hear the will of Nippon, and to understand the might of the Emperor. Those who had taken over the little island had no time to show patience. There was an alternative for those who did not promptly appear.

Bia[1] was one of these, a chief who lived in the north. Not only was he the senior chief of his village, but he was also assistant to the paramount chief, a man of considerable importance. He was a strong supporter of the Methodist Mission, and his elder son was training for mission work.

It chanced that when the Japanese invaded Buka a little handful of Australian soldiers were cut off, and in danger of capture. Bia came to their aid; somehow he managed to keep them in hiding until they could make their way to the larger island of Bougainville. His action soon became known to the Japanese authorities installed on the little island of Sohana, and a price was put on his head. Chief Bia became a fugitive, and as the weeks passed, they hunted him relentlessly. Eventually, he was captured.

Would Bia disclose the new hiding-place of the Australians? Not a word would he speak. And neither the cajolery nor the threats of his captors could move him; but Bia's thoughts were active. Seizing an opportune moment, he eluded his guards and leaped over a cliff. Alas, instead of striking the deep water some thirty feet below, he crashed on to the coral rocks at the water's edge.

Bia lay at the foot of that cliff a poor, broken thing. Hours passed. Eventually the Japanese came to where he was. Once more they had their officers question him. Once more he might be allowed to escape, if escape was his choice. But not one word would he permit himself to utter that would in any way endanger the lives of those he had helped to escape. Broken in body, he was not to be broken in loyalty, choosing rather to give his life.

Then and there his body was drenched in kerosene, and ignited. Not even to the poor charred remains were his captors to show respect; *but those who know this epic of loyalty will honour Bia's name for ever*.

[1] Beer.

And along with Bia, men will remember Luké Zalé. Luké was also summoned to the little island of Sohana. Luké was the senior teacher on the island of Petats, some distance away, where with three others he ministered to three or four hundred of his people. He found himself under armed guard. He was already a marked man. It had become known to his captors that he had helped a Fijian minister and his wife and family to escape. Quietly he determined, if he could, he would set others of his friends free to escape to Bougainville.

Awaiting an opportune moment, he made a dash for the cliff, with the intention of leaping into the sea. The Japanese guard fired their rifles at him, but happily, they missed. Luké knew his ground too well for easy pursuit. The angry guard searched for him. When at last darkness fell, Luké slipped down from his hiding place, down, down silently into the sea. Making his way deliberately out into the current of the Passage, he managed to make a landing on an island about three miles distant, before he became exhausted.

Rested a little, he struck out once more, gathering all his reserve strength, to cross a difficult stretch of water, the stormy end of the Passage where its swift waters pile high against the wind-driven waves of the ocean. Successfully crossing, Luké landed on the south-west corner of Buka. His next big task was to walk overland to a large shallow lagoon some miles up the coast where were some canoes. From here he made his way to his island home of Petats, some eight miles north. An incredible journey!

On arrival, Luké's first care was to warn his friends of the approach of the Japanese. Immediately they began to make plans for a hurried departure. As men, women, and little children assembled on the beach and embarked in their canoes; there was no looking back if safety was to be reached. Alas, the fortunes of war had broken in upon their peaceful lives!

They skirted the chain of islands which extends some twenty to thirty miles to the south, and then set out across the open sea an equal distance, in time arriving at a tiny outpost of the Mission on the wild coast of Bougainville, where they made a landing through the rolling ocean surf.

Still their journey had not ended; leaving the beach behind, they trekked inland. Hour after hour they pushed ahead, wading streams, scrambling up steep ridges, pushing on through long jungle grass, climbing higher ever higher up into the mountain range. At last they reached their goal, a comparatively safe little mountain village. Here, Luké and his family, with thankful hearts, joined once more with those for whom he had placed his life in danger—their Fijian minister and his family. Always it was *safety last!*

The little island of Sohana will ever witness to the truth that Loyalty is of the spirit that shall never die!

Eight

'Unto the Mountain Tops!'

THE great mountain reared its head into the sky. Mauna Loa was the most feared of the four great volcanoes. From the crater a menacing pall of smoke trailed across the sky. In the fathomless crater burned a lake of molten lava. No wonder the poor, ignorant people of Hawaii[1] shuddered as their priests spoke of the flame-goddess Pélé[2] who dwelt in the heart of the Lake of Fire.

The people of Hawaii, girt by the blue seas, were now Christians, but the new faith was to them so new, that they still trembled when their priests invoked the name of Pélé. Perhaps, after all, Pélé *was* greater than Jehovah. She was certainly uncomfortably near.

'Do not neglect her,' said the fathers. 'If you do, her anger will spill over in boiling lava, with merciless ruin and desolation to all the trees.

'She will pour down her anger into the sea and spoil all your fishing grounds,' said the priests, who were angered themselves, now that the people no longer brought them gifts. 'Great is Pélé,' they said, 'and greatly to be feared.'

But there was one woman who did not fear. She bore herself with regal grace, and her strong, fearless eyes looked out with scorn on the priests of Pélé. The people said to one another, 'It is Kapiolani,[3] the chieftainess!'

'Pélé is powerless!' declared this brown-faced woman,' I will tread the province of Pélé, to the very crater edge where the

---

[1] Hawaii—pronounced—Hah-wye-ee.
[2] Pélé—pronounced—Pay-lay.
[3] Kapiolani—pronounced—Kah-pee-o-la-nee.

stones go up, and she shall not touch me. Jehovah, my God is the great God, and Pélé is as nothing.' The people gazed with fear mingled with admiration. 'My God, Jehovah, made these mountains,' added Kapiolani, 'and the lava too; He is the only strong One.'

So the chieftainess Kapiolani would defy the goddess Pélé who lived in the boiling crater, and ruled their island!

Eighty of her people avowed themselves willing to go with her as she climbed the lower valleys filled with trees, up and up till she stood on the scoria and the very crater-edge where Pélé threatened to blast with her fiery breath.

As the party ascended, Kapiolani bent and broke off a branch of a low bush with red and yellow berries. Every one knew that these were Pélé's berries. Of old they had been taught that no one dare touch them without asking her. Not only had the daring Kapiolani broken off the branch to carry with her, but she had actually eaten the berries. The people feared that this was carrying her daring a little too far. Certainly no harm had overtaken her as yet. Still, there was time.

The full natural terrors of the crater came into view. The uncertain ground trembled beneath her feet, the dense cloud of smoke rose into the air. Even Kapiolani was awed. She did not hesitate. The ground was hot with hidden fires, but she had come to defy the heathen goddess.

Would Pélé reach out her finger and slay her? The people waited. Then from her robe Kapiolani drew forth a copy of the New Testament, and there, with ringing voice, she read within hearing of the heathen goddess, if such should be, the message of the one true God.

The people witnessed Kapiolani do this thing that made their hearts to tremble. Then they saw her step down to the edge of the crater and let herself down over the side.

The sulphurous fumes rose about her. There she stood, unafraid. Then they watched her take up the berries and cast them down into the fiery heart of the volcano. Defiantly she sent hurtling down stone after stone. There was no further insult that could be heaped on Pélé. Would she rise in her anger and consume? Nothing happened. Surely she would not let this insult pass. The people waited. Still nothing happened. Kapiolani stood, a solitary figure offering prayer and praise to her God, Jehovah, the maker of the fiery-hearted volcano, and source of her own courage.

Kapiolani rejoined her party. Calling on them to bear her witness of God, she led them in His praise. *And there, that day, for the first time since Creation, the praise of Kapiolani's God rang out across the mountain crater—the song of a free people, no longer subject to the greed of the priests and their mountain goddess.*

Nine

Three Men on a Raft

THE sea looked so flat and solid from the air, but now it was a reaching, greedy thing that shook its prey before devouring it. Our small three-man scout bomber would not float long, we knew.

The sinking of that plane was like a magician's trick. It was there, and then it was gone, and there was nothing left in our big, wet, darkening world but the three of us and a piece of rubber that was not yet a raft. Of course the plane took with it everything the two boys in their well-disciplined haste had pulled together from the emergency stores and equipment. What fight we were to make for our lives must depend upon the junk in our pockets, tools attached to the raft, which were negligible, and the uses we could make of the clothes upon our backs.

Finally I got the raft blown up, but the thing inflated itself upside down. By this time we had been floundering and coughing in the water for quite a while, and we were all exhausted. It was quite dark now, but out eyes were becoming accustomed to it. . . . Gene spoke first. 'There's a way to get this thing over,' he said, still a little short of breath. 'We've got to stop and dope us out a scheme.' Tony chimed in, 'All right.' So we tied the blouses together as Tony had suggested, worked around to the other side and pulled, and boom!—over she came, with a homely thwack on the water.

As we huddled together in the darkness, trying to keep warm while the wind held our clammy clothes against us, we were not downhearted. I had confidence in the raft's ability to stay afloat, and the boys were sure we should be rescued in the morning. (The raft was only eight feet long by four feet wide; the dimensions inside were eighty inches by forty inches. We discovered almost at once that it was impossible for three men to dispose this space so that any one of us would be comfortable.)

If we weren't found to-day, they agreed, help would surely come to-morrow. But I was not so sure. I was an old hand in this business. After all, we were at war. We were in the vicinity of known enemy positions and naval forces. There would be one quick look, and then we must be given up for lost.

A moment came when I thought the boys were right and I was wrong, to my great relief. At first I thought it was a bird, but, far away as it was, we could see that it was steady on its course, and in a few minutes we heard the faint sound of engines. We jumped to our feet in our excitement, and almost tipped over the raft. There was not a single thing that we could use as a signalling device, except our shirts. Gene and Tony already had theirs off and were waving them wildly. Their voices were becoming hoarse. The plane came closer and closer, until she was within half a mile of us. Now she was going away, now the sound of her motors dwindling to the southward like the last note of a dirge.

The boys sank down, their faces expressionless. I have been sorry that I said what I did then: 'Boys, there goes our one and only chance.'

We didn't do a lot of talking that night, but discussed our predicament. All the necessary tools—oars, pump, and so forth —were missing. We found that all that we had was this: a police whistle, a small mirror and a pair of pliers, another pair of pliers which I had stuck in my pocket, and which broke the first time I attempted to use them, an ordinary pocket-knife, a can of rubber cement patching fluid, a small piece of patching material, a ·45 calibre pistol, three clips of ammunition, two pneumatic life-jackets and the clothing we had on. The two lads threw their shoes away, as I was afraid shoes would graze the boat, and also because we needed the space. I kept my shoes;

if we made a desert island we shouldn't want to be entirely without shoes.

'We'll keep a watch,' I said, 'watch on, watch off, and relax between.' Each little wave that struck the bottom of our rubber bubble of a boat was a jarring blow across the shoulders and the back of the head of the man lying inside.

'Hey, look—it's dawn!' The geography of this part of the Pacific was far from a mystery to me. We were without rudder, oars, or canvas, but still I was determined to sail the raft if I could. A serious lack was head covering; the sun's rays came down like red-hot corkscrews and cooked our brains. Tony had his dungaree jacket, so I took his shirt and tore out the two front panels. With these I fashioned a sort of bonnet which gave the top of our heads some protection from the tropical sun. There was no way to protect our faces. Our clothes were constantly drenched. Within fifteen minutes after a good dousing they would be thoroughly dry again.

We thought it was going to be easy to shoot a bird. All day they coasted slowly over our heads, always approaching up wind, and peering curiously down at this odd-looking floating object that had invaded their exclusive world of wind and water.

'We've got to be all for one and one for all,' I explained, 'but when a final decision has to be made by one of us for us all, the captain's word has got to be law.' Tony and Gene, good sailors both, readily assented, and we had no trouble on that score. I kept warning the boys to be careful about fraying or inadvertently snagging the fabric with any sharp metal, or the buttons on their clothes.

Sharks were always near the boat. I have heard many arguments as to whether a shark would attack a human being in the water, but I did not feel that we should take chances. From time to time one of us would offer bits of his life-history, but mostly we talked of food.

On our third day I discovered that I had a pencil. It suddenly burst upon me that this was a marvellous tool. I could make a chart! I knew the approximate position where we had gone into the sea. I traced the lines of latitude and longitude on the front of the life-jacket. 'There's where we are, and there's where we're going,' I said enthusiastically. We could conceivably be driven in vast circles, far from the narrow shipping lanes, until our rubber-and-cloth ship rotted. When this happened, we should long have become three white skeletons.

We were very anxious to work westward from our starting position, and now this new wind was driving us north and east, exactly the opposite of our desires. A good stiff wind in the wrong direction could push this forty-pound boat——

Then I had it! Why wouldn't it be feasible to rig some sort of sea-anchor, check our progress when the wind was wrong? 'Gimme that life-jacket,' I ordered Gene. The half-inch manila rope life-line still encircled the boat. I removed it, and tied one end to the deflated life-jacket, the other to the gas inductor manifold on the pointed bow of the boat. As the jacket sank in the sea and the boat pulled to the end of her tether, the tiny craft jerked, slowed, and swung about lazily, pointing her bow into the wind. Perfect!

Once more the night arrived surprisingly as always in this latitude. We watched the great red sun sink in silence. We felt lonely. Behind us a star gleamed. 'Well, Henry,' Tony said promptly, 'time to put on the pot.'

In a few hours I would make the fifth pencil mark on the gunwale. Five days without food or water. Five days, and three of us crowded together. Five days with no sleep by night, and a pitiless torture by day. Five days of turning our suffering skins, like basting fowl, to baths of stinging salt. Five days—and how many days ahead?

Before evening the three of us were sitting dejectedly silent. Then Gene made a suggestion. 'It might be a good idea,' he said, not meeting our eyes, 'to say a prayer.' We discussed this seriously. We found that we had all been reared in some religious atmosphere, but that we had all drifted away. We all concluded that a word of prayer wouldn't hurt anything. So we sat in the steaming little cup that our boat had become and bowed our heads beneath the cruel tropic sun. We each mumbled a few words of our own awkward choosing, calling on God to bless our loved ones back home, over whom we were more concerned than ourselves, and asking for a little rain.

That night it rained.

The wind picked up in a low roar, and for perhaps five minutes we had a blinding, equatorial deluge. The boat sang with the sound of its beating on the drum-tight sides. We were ducking our heads like greedy fishing birds to suck up each precious mouthful as fast as it collected. As for hunger—our shrunken stomachs were numb now. Then the prayer for rain having worked so well, we decided to ask for food, and incidently a little more rain. Everything we had of metal was rusting badly by now. The pocket-knife and pliers we scraped and polished as best we could.

I was not very enthusiastic when Gene announced he was going to try to stab a fish with a pocket-knife. He would lean out over the boat, poised and ready. I was watching Gene's manœuvres warily. If the boat got punctured we should be in a bad way. One fish was especially curious. Gene stabbed viciously. His knife caught the fish right amidships. Tony lay on the fish until it stopped struggling. 'Come on—lemme scale it,' Gene said, reaching out his hand. Then he handed the knife to me. 'You divide it, chief.' I cut the fish into three equal pieces. 'I never ate raw fish before,' Gene said, a little squeamishly. Each of us gnawed off a small bite. We had no saliva in our mouths, and trying to masticate the raw fish was like chewing gum. The moist innards went down a little better. 'The liver's good for you,' I said, and divided this organ among us. It was poor fare for our first meal in seven days. After we had eaten as much as we could, there was a sizeable portion left. This I wrapped in one of the rags I had torn from Tony's shirt. I stored it in the bow of the boat. 'There's a meal for later,' I said.

That day it rained again. I hit upon the idea of soaking the rain-water up in rags. This time we were prepared. We wrung our clothes over the side, and put them on refreshed.

I had been lying on my back for perhaps a half-hour, my eyes closed, when there was a terrific explosion. Gene had shot an albatross. The bird had alighted on the stern about six inches above my head. Gene and Tony were yelling, 'Get him! Get him! Don't let him get away!' The bird's carcase was drifting slowly away. Instantly I dived over the side. Whether I was strong enough to swim, and the possibility of getting back never occurred to me. I was back on board before the boat had drifted twenty feet. Naturally we recalled the Ancient Mariner's curse. I knew that all seamen since olden times have held the albatross in great awe, and believed it sacred.

My watch came round about midnight. It was very dark. Sitting awhile, I noticed a glow of light in the bow. It seemed to be coming from our pile of rags. I got down and untangled the rags until I came upon the meat we had saved from the fish, and the carcase of the albatross. They were strongly phosphorescent. I aroused the boys. 'Look's like it's spoiled all right,' Tony said slowly. 'I don't know about you fellas,' he said, 'but I wouldn't feel like eating any more of that.' The rest of the night passed uneventfully.

After destroying all our food-supply, we were worried about getting some more. Then Gene caught a shark, using the knife like a hook. We had another prayer-meeting that night, and every night thereafter. Each evening, after the sun's flamboyant departure left us feeling more alone in a world that had suddenly lost all colour, we devoted perhaps an hour to our informal service. There was a comfort in passing our burden to some one bigger than we in this empty vastness. I hadn't been to church for years, so it's easy to imagine how good I was at recalling the stories I had learned as a youngster. Gene recalled a number of stories, but couldn't tell them. Tony had never heard any of these things before. Well, I didn't want to tell everything I knew in one night, so each evening I'd tell one story. That went on until the end.

The wind had lightened when Gene's second watch came round. Gene wet his finger and held it up to test the wind. 'Ain't hardly no breeze at all,' he said. He leaned over the side and dipped his hand in the water to see if he could feel any drift. His fingers had no sooner got into the water than he let out an agonized yell. A grey shape flung itself from his hand and went into the water on the opposite side, with such a splash. I was impatient for the first light of dawn, so I could examine the finger closely. The hand was badly lacerated. Tooth-marks showed plainly. The shark—if shark it was—had raked down his index finger, cutting almost completely through the nail in two places. I began to realize how badly we needed some sort of medical kit. We had a lot of trouble with our lips. Stinging salt-water baths, which we could not avoid, continually irritated the cracked and blistered flesh.

Time after time we would no sooner get the boat free than a high green comber would curl down upon us, half-filling the boat with churning foam. Here we had the feeling, for the first time, of being hand-to-hand against the sea. There was no time to think of hunger; that gnawing pain was now becoming part of us. The comforts and discomforts brought by rain had become routine. We didn't talk so often now.

'Hey, we must be near land, chief.' It was Tony who spoke suddenly. 'Look at that junk,' he said. Bits of debris floated on the hot blue waves, wet sticks glinting. 'Suppose we do hit an island—might be a desert island,' Tony suggested. 'A desert island would be better than no island at all,' Gene answered him. We discussed the possibilities.

The fifteenth day dawned on a torpid sea. As the morning wore on I saw no signs of the calm lifting. Finally my eyes lit upon my shoes, which I was still saving. 'Gene,' I said, 'give me the knife.' With the knife I cut away the uppers. I moved over to the forward thwart, sat down and tried it out. 'Glory be!' I whispered. It worked exactly like a small canoe paddle, except that my arm was the handle. In a few minutes I had made another 'paddle'. When the boys saw that my idea would work, their listlessness vanished. All that day we rowed, never stopping, until about two o'clock the next morning—almost eighteen hours. The next day, however, we lost all that we had gained.

Tony was lying down. It was getting to be about the time of day when the equatorial sun seemed to take on a positive malevolence. Suddenly Tony sat up. 'I feel a coconut,' he said. Gene and I watched him stupidly. Was Tony imagining things? 'I felt a coconut bump me under the bottom of the boat.' I jumped up, and looked over the side. Sure enough, there was a coconut bobbing just out of reach. Soaked as it was, the outer shell was easy to remove. I tasted the milk inside. Our systems needed oil. Twenty-one days in the sun of the tropics had boiled the moisture out of our bodies.

On the twenty-fifth day we had a terrifying experience. An ominously rolling mass, almost jet-black, appeared in the misty grey, and for the first time we heard thunder. The sea was growing dark. The black cloud spat a thin stream of electric flame, long, thin and forked. Like a great slap in the face the rain fell. And the next instant we were in the water, the raft flying over our heads. I made a wild grab for the rags. I was considerably worried over what might have gone in the tip-over.

We lay some time, recuperating slowly. Our minds were growing dull. 'Hey, boys,' I called, trying to sound jovial—but I guess I wasn't even fooling myself, 'It's our anniversary! We've been in the water a month—the twenty-eighth day began a minute ago!' On this twenty-eighth day Gene raised the coconut alarm again. We thought we must be nearing land. The winds were variable, and generally high. The squalls were cold now—miserably cold, and we huddled together to keep warm.

The sea is cunning. It can bide its time. The wind was its ally. The raft tipped over. We were in the sea again. Some time later, maybe hours, I took the inventory. All our spare rags were gone. We passed the night in misery in the brewing hurricane.

On the thirty-second day we got a shift of wind. It rained often during the night. We got up to bail and wring out our clothes again.

A new day came. The raft was bobbing like an orange rind. 'Let's take a sun-bath before we put our clothes on,' I suggested. Next moment there was a wild scramble, mad grasping, and a confusion of shouts. 'The clothes! The clothes!' I yelled frantically. The scornful wind snatched the words, and a great wave engulfed me. The raft was upside down. Now all our clothes were lost—every thread and stitch, except, ridiculously, a police whistle that hung by a cord around my neck.

We topped a wave on the thirty-fourth morning, and Gene spoke for the first time since taking the watch. 'Chief,' he said, 'I see a beautiful field of corn.' I didn't even look up. I thought sadly that the boy's mind had finally gone. When we had risen to the next crest he spoke again insistently, 'Sure, enough chief. I see something green in the distance!' I looked hard, but could still see nothing in the tumbling sea. I couldn't stand on my cramped and crooked legs. I asked the boys to hold me upright. I instantly recognized it as an island, one of the low verdant atolls of the far South Sea. I let out a hoarse whoop. 'Well!' Gene said, 'thank God—and it's about time.'

Chartless, we had no idea what the island was. I took a bearing on the island, compared it with the wind direction, and found that our coarse of drift was carrying us about ten degrees to the right. I took the port side of the raft, using our one remaining shoe-paddle. Gene and Tony paddled together on the starboard side, using their hands only. We rowed all day.

At first we thought there was only one island; as we approached we saw that there were two, with a wide gap of water between. There was still the uncertainty that this might be in the Japanese Mandate.

We came in closer, perhaps within three miles of the curving beach. 'Chief,' Gene said, 'those aren't rocks on the beach. They're shacks.' 'Wishful thinking, Gene,' I said. They still look like rocks to me.'

The waves were very high and we could see the island only when we came to the crest. We were completely exhausted. The nearer we approached the reef, the larger the breakers looked. The crest began to curl dangerously. There was a roar like a cannon-shot as the mass of water smashed. Our only hope was to paddle over the reef ahead of the breaker—in the interval between two waves.

The breaker caught the raft behind. When we saw it next it was speeding landward like a chip before the surf. The three of us were in the water. I can remember spinning head over heels three or four times, and raking along the floor of the sea. Afterwards I discovered that a patch of skin about six inches in diameter had been scraped from the centre of my back. Gene and Tony were going through the same thing. I heard a call for help. It was from Tony. Being unable to swim, he thought he was going to drown. On all fours, we dragged ourselves from the last persistent clutch of the sea, and somehow hauled the raft behind us. To me, terribly dizzy from exhaustion, the world seemed to be spinning round us. We were too weak to try to find food.

We decided to rest for the night in one of the shacks. I thought it must have stood there for a long time. Whilst looking about in the rafters I found a thick book in a strange language. It developed that this was a native Bible.

Next morning we saw a native coming towards us from the beach. It was obvious that he couldn't understand our being there. In a few minutes he was back with several coconut kernels. As we ate, the native made signs that he was going for help. We looked at each other in relief. At least the natives were friendly.

He returned later with a party of several natives and a man who turned out to be the resident commissioner. The first native recognized from our eyes that we were white man; by our burned skins he could not tell whether we were white, brown, yellow, red, or black. The commissioner was curious as to how we had reached this particular part of the island. He was astounded. No one had ever come over that reef and lived to tell the tale!

The natives carried us a mile or more until we arrived at the commissioner's residence.'

❦   ❦   ❦

And so to safety! A miracle of the sea! In thirty-four long days and nights!

A greater miracle when it is realized that in choosing that one of the two visible islands as their objective, they had chosen the only inhabited island within many hundreds of miles; they had come in over the reefs deemed impossible by the natives who knew their island, they had dragged themselves for the first night's rest into the only inhabited hut around, and had escaped from the grim terrors of the sea only a matter of hours before the most devastating hurricane in living memory struck the islands, wrecking and threshing all in its course for three days!

A miracle of the sea!

Ten

'Jericho Road'

The ways of the world are full of haste and turmoil:
I will sing of the tribe of helpers who travel in peace.

ALL looked quiet and peaceful. Bees were busy in the flowers, and gaily-coloured parrots rested in the shade of the tropical palms. The warm sun sparkled on the blue waters of the little harbour where several boats bobbed about restlessly at anchor.

It was a bright scene. But the German priest who was walking slowly in the Mission garden was troubled. He knew of the terrible warfare going on in another part of the country. Each day would bring news of jungle battle, and he thought of the wounded and dying. He knew only too well how impossible it would be for men to find their way through the thick jungle that crouched all round the little Mission settlement; and there were the fevers that came from poison pools, plants, and insects. He sighed as he lifted his hand, and shading his eyes, looked towards the dense, cruel tangle of trees.

Surely those figures—one, two, three, four—were not men. Surely they were only trees swaying in the breeze. He strained his eyes to see more clearly. But as they came closer he saw that they were men—and his country's enemies. In a moment he stood beside them. They were exhausted. He saw now that they were Australians. Somehow, he got them to the Mission House. They were wounded, starved, and half-dead with malaria. They had walked and walked, hacking their way through the awful jungle, living on wild berries and sharing the last drop of the precious water which they carried.

∾　　∾　　∾

For days the German priest nursed and fed them, thinking of nothing but the needs and comforts of sick men.

At last the soldiers were well enough to walk abroad and to begin to make plans for escape. The sea was the biggest difficulty. How could they get a boat?

They tried to keep their plans from the priest who had befriended them. They were not sure, even yet, how far they should trust him. Imagine their surprise then when one evening he came to them and said, 'There will be a boat in the harbour for you to-night. You will know what to do.'

The four soldiers looked at one another. This little German priest was running great risks to help them. They did not know how to thank him. And they were his enemies! One of the Australians burst out, 'Father, you had better come with us. If any one finds out what you have done you will lose your life. Come with us.'

The priest shook his head. 'No, my brothers, I will not come. My place is here, and I am not afraid. I obey the law of my Master who said, "Love your enemies". Good-bye, and may God guide you.' *With that, he turned, and went into his Mission House, a German priest, who had made the story of the Good Samaritan of the Jericho Road happen in the jungle of New Guinea!*

Eleven

An Eye for a Life

THE white woman stood in the Japanese park. Already she knew just enough of the strange language to be able to tell er wonderful story.

Then suddenly, she was aware only of a blinding pain. Her ye had gone. A young hooligan, half-hidden among the bushes, ad thrown a stone.

The police tried to find him when it was seen what damage he ad done. But Miss Imhoff would hear no suggestions that he ould be punished. The police had not often met people who ook this attitude. It was already evident to them that the in-red woman would never use her eye again.

       ❧   ❧   ❧

Years rolled by, and one day there came into Nagasaki har-our, a Japanese man-o'-war. The local Christians rallied to give 1e officers and men a reception.

The captain of the ship himself replied to the words of wel-ome that preceded the banquet, surprising everybody present y telling them that he too was a Christian. Then he told how e had become one. Years before, he confessed, he had thrown stone at a lady missionary in one of Nagasaki's parks, and put ut one of her eyes. In great cowardice he had fled to the moun-ains, managing to hide himself there for three days. Then news ame to him that the woman whom he had injured did not wish o have him punished—that she had forgiven him, and was raying that he might become Christian. It was so unusual that e could not get it out of his mind. With the passing of days he read everything he could about Christianity to try to understand why it made people like that. He thought and prayed, and in time he became Christian.

And now, he was glad, he declared with radiant face, to be able to say these things in the very city where he first learned what it was to be a Christian.

Miss Imhoff was there, and heard—and deeply moved, rejoiced that years before she had had the grace to follow Him who when He had lost infinitely more, had prayed: '*Father, forgive them, for they know not what they do.*'

So does the glorious Kingdom of the Christ come to the hearts of men!

Twelve

'One of the Little Ships'

To get away was becoming hourly more difficult. Two
years of war in Europe had left the islands of the Solomon
Group practically untouched. Now it was a different story. The
Japanese were on the way. The collection of Mission buildings
at Munda would be an early target, and there were missionary
women—two of them just out of sick-beds. The decision to get
the women-folk away must be made at once if at all. The doctor
and one of the sisters had already paddled off in a canoe to confer
with a distant planter.

All day long hurried and uncertain plans were made. News
came that Kieta had fallen. Something must be done without
delay. Some of the party, at the moment, were separated by
miles.

When at last the *Fauro Chief* was ready to cast off, her crew
comprised a doctor, a trader, a planter, an old and sick man who
had been a ship's officer thirty years before, and six women. As
long as they lived they would never forget that hour when they
faced each other. Native boys accompanied the amateur sailors
through the difficult Marovo Lagoon. All were tired. The last
days and nights had been full.

The tiny vessel of nineteen tons, measuring only fifty-four
feet in length, and thirteen across at midships, offered little space
in which to crowd eleven people, most of them prostrate in the
early part of the voyage. There were only two bunks—
sketchily-made 'shake-downs' on the deck and hatches served
for the rest of the party.

A hurried call was made at a plantation, the residence of an
old islander. Before parting he gave the crew his sextant, some

navigation books and a general chart of the Pacific—the only chart they were able to get; but he shook his head over the project, saying they might be months on the way.

The native boys had come to where they must turn back. The amateurs were alone now, to face whatever might be coming to them. Now the tiny boat was tackling the open sea. By mid-afternoon, the hill-tops behind were a blue haze on the horizon—the last land they were to see for many terrifying days and nights.

Soon they were bucking into the teeth of a stiff wind, with short choppy seas of a most disagreeable kind. The women tackled the galley, the men tested out their seamanship. Two of the women even took turns at the wheel. There was work for every one fit to stand.

Night came. They ran into a tropical thunderstorm. Some of the beds were drenched.

Next day brought a head-wind and big seas, hindering the progress. The jibs were called into use, the course altered slightly. All the afternoon they battled on. One of the women had recovered from seasickness enough to act as stewardess.

A hot meal was planned before dark—no easy thing to plan in a rough sea. The wife of the planter stood in the galley aft, cup in hand, holding a good saucepan of hot soup. Suddenly, a cry went up: 'Man overboard!—at least, woman overboard!' And she was unable to swim a stroke! In a moment her husband had jumped in to her rescue—and he was the tiny crew's only engineer!

They did the wrong things first. The old boatman issued orders that nobody could hear. The two overboard, visibly exhausted, were unable to clutch the life-belt thrown to them. Could they last out? There were no minutes to spare. Then the last remaining man on board, not fully occupied, jumped in. A second life-belt was thrown. Only at the end of what seemed like hours, were three exhausted and considerably shaken people dragged aboard.

Some days of fine weather followed this nerve-wracking experience—as if to compensate—calm seas, and a breeze to fill the jibs. Before the weather could change, the crew marked the Sunday with a brief service—the congregation a mixed one, several Methodists, a Seventh Day Adventist, an Anglican and a Roman Catholic.

The real dangers were now ahead. Reefs! Seven days out, the little vessel was realized to be off her course. Breakers on both bows—and less than half a mile away—greeted the crew as an alarming spectacle at daybreak!

All that day was spent in vainly seeking an opening through to the open sea. By nightfall, the little vessel rounded what appeared to be the end of the reef. Safety seemed at hand.

Then disaster took the crew by grim surprise. With a terrific impact, they grounded on a sunken reef! The shock, in itself, seemed enough to shatter the little *Fauro Chief*; her bows high and dry, and stern almost under water. The prospect was not a happy one. Yet, as if by a miracle, not a leak of any kind developed! After an hour of anxious manœuvring the little craft was eased off into deep water again. A sigh of relief went up from the crew.

A conference was speedily called. The vessel was set about, with engines dead slow, and every possible watch kept, but in spite of this, within the hour she was up again—this time with both bow and stern aground. With every wave she grounded and wrenched, the heavy tropical rains soaked everything; thunder and lightning added to the discomfort. Search from the dingy aided by the lead-line, failed to reveal any water deeper than a fathom. Australia seemed a long, long way off in that moment! Not daring to remain so precariously situated, the engine was started up, and with perilous grindings and bumpings, the little vessel was actually manœuvred right across the platform of the reef and down into the water on the other side. Three fathoms! Three and a half, four fathoms! Too good to be true! With sighs of relief, the crew cast anchor, and set themselves to wait for the morning.

Morning revealed the little vessel anchored within a wide semicircle of sheltering reef. Outside, tremendous seas continued to pound. On the horizon waves were breaking into foam on wider and wider circles of reef, and only to the westward was there any sign of open water. At times, heavy squalls completely reduced the visibility. It was apparent that they must stay where they were until the weather cleared—just how long, nobody knew.

The days passed—the first, and the second, and the third, and the fourth! Always night brought the gale stronger and more threatening. Teeming rain fell.

On the second Sunday out, the storm actually reached the height of its fury. The tiny vessel strained at her anchor until it seemed that something must go. Something did go. She began to drift; in a short time she was in the thick of it again—dragging forty fathoms of chain! Tossed like a cork, her crew was driven to wondering just how much longer she could hold out. The anchor-shackle had already parted.

All that Sunday their plight looked desperate. In the afternoon, after a brief respite, they faced an equally fierce blow from the opposite direction—their tiny vessel the toy-thing of the furies.

No one knew exactly where they were. Just on dark, creaming breakers ahead, revealed what they had been preserved from during the long hours of helplessness.

The doctor had made some effort to establish their position, but from his reading, they appeared to be then in the centre of Australia! It seemed there must be some little mistake! The vessel was put about, and they spent the whole of the night in cautious sailing to and fro—an hour each way—till a new day would bring them opportunity to seek a passage through the treacherous reefs. In time the moon rose to cheer their watch, and to guide them through the hours till dawn.

Morning brought relief. Sunshine! Gentle breezes! A way through the reefs appeared. Soaked mattresses and clothes were spread on deck. Everybody was up and about, save the lady member of the crew who had been overboard. Sunshine at last, and calm seas, made it possible to take an accurate reading of the position.

A tiny island appeared on the horizon! Land! Pine Island it proved to be—sixty miles from the Australian coast. And there at last they found sheltered anchorage, and a lighthouse. For the first time in weeks the whole crew had a good night's sleep.

'Where have you come from?' the men at the lighthouse wanted to know at once.

'We've come from the Solomons,' they answered.

'Don't put that across us,' was the reply they got, 'nobody ever came from the Solomons that way, and in that bit of a thing.'

But they had. They had come eleven hundred miles, through reef-bound seas; they had wrestled with phenomenal storms. Nor was there a soul on board who failed to marvel at their preservation.

On the following Wednesday they made Mackay, on the Australian coast. Only then did they hear a moving story. On the previous Sunday—when they had been in such dire straits—a minister at this place had been conducting morning worship at West Mackay. When he was about to pronounce the benediction at noon, a strange compulsion was laid upon him to pray for the missionaries in the Solomons. He did not know any of them; their work was not even a charge upon his Church; but he and his people remained to pray.

And the following Wednesday it was to this very place that the little mission boat, Fauro Chief *came!* A spontaneous thanksgiving service was arranged by the minister and his people. *As all avowed, it was the crowning of an experience which meant a deepening of faith for all.*

Thirteen

The God in the Basket

CREAMS reached the ears of the good Sister as she was tending her brown family, 'Mother! Mother! Quick! Dalekala!' She put down the little babe she was feeding, and ran in the direction of the cry. The name of Dalekala was enough. With heart a-thumping, Sister Ethel McMillan was across the stream. There was Dalekala dragging one of her girls up the hill.

Something of a law unto himself, he was a huge fellow of vile temper, and greatly feared by the people. He had strenuously opposed the spread of the Gospel on Choiseul. Already he had two wives, and of late had cast his eyes on a third. But she was a young relative, and therefore *tabu* for him. He had actually taken the girl, but she had run away to seek refuge in Sister Ethel's Home. Very angry, Dalekala had vowed that he would come and take her back.

He came, and prowling round with shield and axe for many weeks, he watched until he had a good idea of the routine of the Girls' Home. He knew the hour at which they rose, the hour at which they settled for the night, such times as they went to the sea to bathe, and to the stream to wash.

This morning, the girl of his seeking had set off to the stream to wash clothes. Dalekala watching closely, grabbed her. Mercifully, her cries were heard. Some of the older girls ran to her aid. Presently Sister appeared on the scene, and then the real struggle began—each hanging on to the poor girl. In this manner several hours passed.

A suggestion was then made that the girls go and blow the conch shell. Realizing that something was wrong, those at work in the gardens hurried to the spot of battle. Of course, they found Sister struggling with Dalekala. They at once surrounded the contending parties. The boys suggested tying up Dalekala, and taking him to Gizo, the Government Station, but Sister would agree to nothing of the kind. 'No, oh, no,' she said, 'we must not think of doing any such thing. Besides, we hope to win Dalekala.'

So they continued to keep the ring round the party. Then they began to pray. *They prayed there in turns for five hours*—with their eyes open, of course! And God got a lot of information about Dalekala's character that day—more than he would have given of himself in his frankest moments!

As the day wore on, heavy tropical showers drove the contending parties to seek shelter. The old heathen threatened to break the girl's arm; but nothing could deter the good Sister. Dalekala would have to break her own arm first, she said: 'God sent the girl here for me to protect, and what touches her touches me.'

This spiritual third degree proved in the end, too much for Dalekala. It was a battle of spiritual forces. Dalekala exhausted, confessed, 'You win, Sister! You win! Your God is stronger than mine. I carry mine in my basket, but you carry yours in your heart!'

The day was well on. But God had won a great victory that day! Sister was now able to speak to Dalekala of the love and graciousness of God. 'Our God is not like the god of the basket,' she said, 'He will never fail you.'

'I give in,' was Dalekala's broken reply, 'I give in. I am a sinful man. I now give up all idea of this wrong that I have tried to do.'

So a great victory was won that day!

◦◦   ◦◦   ◦◦

Weeks later Dalekala was home once more at Seqa. It was a different Dalekala who was to be seen helping load the *Tandanya*, the Mission boat. He appeared laughing and happy.

Many and many a time in the hard, joyous days of the years following, as she set herself to her big task, Sister Ethel McMillan was to remember that challenge: 'You win, Sister. You win. Your God is stronger than mine. *I carry my god in a basket, but you carry yours in your heart!*'

Fourteen

'Sign of the Number One Man!'

THE black men paused in their digging. 'Why are we digging this pit, *Bapa*?' they asked.

'We are going to erect a *Marian*'—a sacred totem pole—answered their white friend.

'A *Marian*? But if we put it here on the headland the women and the children will see it.'

'Yes,' answered their friend, 'but this is the totem of Jesus—every one may look at it, the women and the children as well as the men. It is the biggest totem of all; it is His mark—we call it His cross.'

So they returned to their digging.

In time the cross was raised; hand-squared from a swamp tree, and about forty feet high, it stood on the Yirrkala headland, towering over the native camps and the Mission. All who came to Yirrkala now, by bush track or canoe, would know that they were coming to the place of the cross.

With the visible cross on the cliff face, the missionary found himself thinking it would be easier to talk about the real Cross to these people whose minds were steeped in symbolism. Primitives, they lived so much in the past—their tribal history, beliefs, and myths all linked to some visible momento, or totemic-centre. The missionary knew well how they guarded their sacred sites, their rocks, pools, trees.

For five years now they had heard daily at Morning Prayers, day school and Sunday services the story of Jesus. How natural then to speak to them in the language that they knew, and say of this towering cross on the headland, 'This is the

totem of Jesus'—His Cross—and pointing to it, with the simple
story of mercy on his lips, say, 'God loves you like that!'

❧   ❧   ❧

Some years of war have passed since that cross was put up on
the headland. Now there is a wonderful sequel. A young
American pilot, Clarence S. Sandford, found himself in difficulties, and forced to bail out into the lonely waters of North
Australia. Somehow he managed to strike out and swim the
three miles to an island, where he collapsed on the beach.

Hours passed; slowly he opened his eyes. He wondered where
he was. Two naked aboriginals stood over him, one of them
pressing a spear-point into his chest. Was he still delirious?

'You Jap?' asked the aboriginal.

'No!' he replied.

The word conveyed very little to the dark man with the spear.
With a scowl he cowered over the exhausted man. The young
airman could find no comfort in the jabbering tongues.

Then suddenly a change flashed across the face of the dark man
who stood above with the spear. His eyes fastened on a little
silver cross that the young airman was wearing. Dropping his
spear, he exclaimed in broken bushman English, '*Jesus, Number
One Man!*'

Next moment the two dark men were helping Sandford to his
unsteady feet. They saw how weak he was; they brought him
fruit. Eventually, they brought him with great tenderness to the
Mission Station at Yirrkala.

The airman, wearing still the little silver cross, was now in
sight of the great white cross towering on the headland. *And in
that moment he knew that it was that cross—known to these dark
men as the Totem of Jesus—that alone had called them back to
something merciful.*

Fifteen

'From Heart to Heart'

THE little child Tarore was back. There was great joy in her
father's heart. He, the proud Ngakuku, had allowed her to
go over the great blue ranges to Tauranga to learn the *pakeha's*
ways from Mrs. Brown and the good Archdeacon there. Now
she was back, and his heart was glad.

Little Tarore, though shy, had made good progress, and when
she was about to leave for home, Mrs. Brown had given her for
her own a little copy of St. Luke's Gospel. Every day since her
return she had carried it in a Maori kit hung round her neck.
Nor would she be parted from it even at nightfall. And in the
long evenings, between sundown and the coming of the darkness, she read to her father.

As her father listened, a strange, new wonder came over him.
He knew that it was more than the voice of his little child that he
heard. 'Why, these,' he said, 'these are the words of the Great
Spirit!' Again and again he listened, and, captivated by what he
heard, he became Christian.

Months later he and his men set out on a journey. They took
little Tarore and her baby brother with them. By evening they
had come to some lovely falls where the great waters came down
over the mountainside in two great leaps of hundreds of feet.
Tired, the party made camp. Thoughtlessly, as they were about
their evening meal, they allowed some smoke to escape through
the tree-tops. It was seen by a war-party from the enemy Arawa
tribe far up the valley.

Very early in the morning the enemy crept down stealthily
through the bush and fell upon the little encampment by the
falls. Roused quickly, the brave Ngakuku gave his orders and

got his party up the hill to safety. But in the confusion, little Tarore was forgotten. Sleeping her childish sleep there by the great falls, she was never to waken again.

Some time later, her sad father risked a return, and carried the little body into a nearby settlement for burial.

Ngakuku's men were wroth when they heard the sad tidings, and called for instant revenge. Ngakuku confessed that he had glimpsed a new way; 'The Great God whom I have learned to love,' he said, 'He will take care of the revenge.' And so it was.

A fortnight later there occurred a further clash between the two parties. This time three of the raiding party were killed. Their chief, Uita, however, escaped unhurt, and carrying with him trophies of the fight, made his way back to Rotorua. Among his trophies was little Tarore's kit with its Maori Gospel.

There it lay unopened for a long, long time. Then one day, a slave named Ripahau came to Rotorua. He had been taught to read by the Mission workers in the north, and with great satisfaction demonstrated his power by reading Tarore's little Gospel. Many gathered to listen. As Ripahau continued to read, a strange thing happened in their midst—old Uita, the raiding chief, whose hands had been stained by the blood of the little owner of the Book, gave his heart and life to the Great God. Almost his first thought was to send word to his one-time enemy, Ngakuku, to tell him the good news. Truly, the God of the little Book had avenged Ngakuku!

The slave, treasuring still his power to read, left Rotorua and travelled down the many miles to Otaki, and joined up there with the warrior Te Rauparaha, the Maori Napoleon, one of the most feared. The famous chief, however, had a son of milder ways. He was anxious for the son to have some of the new learning, and so engaged the newcomer to teach him to read. A cousin of the young man's made up the class of two, with Ripahau the slave as teacher. Lessons began with a few torn pages from an old prayer-book. Interest waned, somewhat, as the pupils progressed, so a messenger was dispatched to Rotorua for more books to read.

When at last they came to hand they were a mixed lot—one among them had completely lost its outside pages and cover. They had been torn off to make bullet-wads; but notwithstanding damage, it was still possible to spell out the name of the one-time owner of the Book, 'NGAKUKU'—*it was Tarore's very Gospel!*

With the passing of time, all three of that strange little reading class became Christian—the slave teacher chiefly through the witness of the other two. Through the new-found Christian faith of the chief's son, Tamihana, a wave of evangelism swept through the *pa*, and through the tribe. Anxious to get a missionary who could teach them yet more, Tamihana set off on a journey many hundreds of miles north to plead their cause. As a result of this perilous journey, a missionary was sent down to Otaki.

Gazing away to the South Island, Tamihana saw there the outline of the land where lived his father's powerful enemies.

As he gazed, he was filled with a great longing to become a missionary to them. So taking with him his cousin—the young man who had learned to read—the two set out in an open canoe. Part of the way was very treacherous. They skirted the great coast of the Kaikouras to Canterbury, thence down to Otago, visiting every *pa*, and reading to the people.

With such success did these two young adventurers set about their task, that when Bishop Selwyn, the first Bishop to New Zealand, went South, he found, as well as the firmly established Methodist Mission, many scores of Maoris who had become Christian through the witness and reading of Tamihana.

Still—so marvellous is the power of God's Spirit through one little Book—the story is not completely told; only recently the British and Foreign Bible Society added a thrilling postscript: 'For several years now,' it said, 'the native children of Otaki, *the direct spiritual descendants of Tamihana*, have been giving money to send Gospels to other children far away.' (They have sent them to Mary Slessor's country, to the little children of Japan, and to the far-away children of Dr. Grenfell's Labrador, and now a letter has come thanking the little Maori children of Otaki for their gift.) What romance!

So continues the story of Tarore's little Gospel—one little Book!

Sixteen

'Dreamers of Dreams'

Was there ever such a general as Jabez Bunting at the head of his storm troops, asking for and expecting implicit obedience? He had certain 'maxims for missionaries' which he was in the habit of rapping out with effect in Missionary Committee, in the middle of the eighteen-hundreds: 'A missionary ought to be willing to live anyhow and to die anywhere.' 'A missionary will not be murdered, though he may be assassinated.' 'All persons taken into work for mission stations, to remain abroad for life.' His recruits should have been men of iron; in reality they were some of the mildest of men. Thomas Adams, from the heart of Cornwall was one of them. In the words of that delectable county, he was 'as easy as an old shoe'. The great God who mounted John Wesley on a horse, embarked Thomas Adams on a windjammer, and saw to it that he was ultimately landed on the coral islands of the South Seas—but that wasn't yet.

Just now everything centred on a farm-house above Laneast town. Bleak it might be, but it gave glorious views of the sea and Dartmoor, even an island far away like a cloud on the horizon. About such a place hung the long half-whisper of the Celt. The gospel that Wesley preached in the eighteenth century exactly met the pensive, prehistoric, emotional gloom. It came as new life to a lost world.

The farm-house was a Methodist stronghold. The father, whose days were filled with grinding work and fluctuating prices, faithfully carried out his practice of leaving all the problems to enter into his closet to pray three times a day. The *eldest* son, John, had seemingly little aptitude for farming. When sent to

E   65

fetch the cows or to see to the sheep on the old gold common, there was no knowing when he would come back. Whilst brother John's dreams were of the stars and the higher mathematics, the nightmares of Thomas were of the soul. Thomas, the *second* son was a dreamer, and sad withal, until the light came. When Christ finally saved him, the chief of sinners, by the might of His Cross, he never forgot the outer darkness. Now, indeed, he knew that he was saved to serve, and so great was his sense of what love had done for him that it only deepened a natural humility.

Jabez Bunting might rebuke his other lieutenants for their propensity for boasting, but for young Thomas Adams his advice was superfluous; never was a more gentle shepherd. Indeed, the hall-mark of the whole Adams family seems to have been humility. Brother John Adams added a new planet to the solar system, not letting his left hand know what his right hand was doing: there was no reason to talk about it, for after all, Neptune had been there all the time, and the priority of knowledge belonged only to God. And in the same spirit Brother Thomas laboured. Scarcely could he allow the Plymouth District Meeting to send his name forward for the ministry, begging for another year in which to make himself more worthy.

When it became evident that eldest son John, would never make a farmer, the whole family had rallied round as one, and with superb faith and courage sent the lad to Cambridge. It had meant heavy work for those left behind on the farm, but they had never so much as thought of complaint. Brother Thomas could not offer for the ministry, or any of them think of anything else but sheep, cows, and corn until John had his degree.

He came home at times. Then the mother supplied the budding mathematician with bowls of bread and milk in his all-night sittings in the farm-house parlour, as he worked at his problems, as incomprehensible to her, as Browning's *Not a fourth sound—but a star.*

But one memorable day an event occurred that she could

understand—it was Squire riding from Launceston market with
a message that her John was the best of all the mothers' sons at
Cambridge. Squire took off his hat and shouted, 'Adams for
ever!' and talked about a Senior Wrangler, which was an out-
andish name for her son, but in the joy of the moment she let
that pass. Soon her husband arrived from the market to confirm
the great news, and to acknowledge with tears of joy that the
Lord had done great things for them whereof they ought to be
glad. The whole family that Saturday afternoon shared the
triumph, which after all, they said, was the Lord's. Of course,
Mother had worked and Father had prayed, and all the children
ploughed and gathered grain in the sweat of their brow for this
glad hour.

The way was now open for young Thomas and his harvesting
of souls. He was accepted for the Methodist ministry, and sent
off to Richmond College. The journey appears to have taken
three days, with a final stage-coach from Southall to Richmond.
Straightway he settled himself in, bought Watson's works, and
visited Greenwich with Brother John. He also saw Jabez
Bunting in the flesh, and underlined the great news in a letter to
the old farm hard by Laneast Common.

Time passed. His training came to an end. Thomas was not
one to overlook the significance of the fact that it was whilst
home helping with the harvest in the vacation time that the great
news arrived of his appointment to the Friendly Isles. He had
only to lift up the eyes of his soul to behold the *field 'white
already unto harvest'*.

But the commands of Jabez Bunting's Missionary Committee
went further; he was ordered to go abroad as a married man.
Poor, humble, Thomas Adams! It could only have been the
thought of the perishing heathen, who would continue to perish
all the time that Thomas Adams looked for a wife, that steadied
the feeble knees and the trembling heart. How could he—shy
Thomas Adams—ask a perfect stranger to marry him, and go
with him where missionaries had been killed by the natives, and

the first missionary's wife drowned in the break-up of a canoe on its way to Vau Vau? There was no doubt about the quality of Jabez Bunting's nerve. A suggestion of a family of some good Methodist girls at Taunton seems to have been added to the injunction. True, they were a high-spirited lot. Jabez Bunting knew the position well. But now the message came to Thomas Adams—try that indomitable French family. Miss French might consent, and so help on this project of the conversion of the heathen. There is something desperately *Methodistic* in looking up the nearest circuit likely to provide a wife at short notice.

Trembling, Thomas Adams set off for Taunton. The local Methodist minister was obliged to tell him that the lady whose name had been circulated to him, was engaged to marry some one else, but he advised him that she had sisters.

At the moment the young ladies were at Burnham-on-Sea, but the parson seems to have been nothing loath to play the part of Cupid; he made up a little parcel—one would hope of Methodist class tickets—for Thomas to take, and thus introduce himself On to Burnham he journeyed, in what state of trepidation one can imagine. God was certainly moving in a mysterious way to get Thomas Adams embarked on his errand.

The young ladies were out when he knocked on the Burnham door. They were taking the air on the beach. The poor caller must have felt like running away, but he proceeded to the sands walking as delicately as Agag before execution. There were the young girls, with auburn tresses blown by the sea breezes and cheeks kissed by the sun. Let us hope they had seen a tall stranger in their teacups that morning. But things worked out So sudden a wooing was no more unlikely than any other plan made by Jabez Bunting, and stage-managed for the benefit of the perishing heathen.

Little Miss Maria French did not lack courage when, within six short weeks, she promised to sail with that same dark stranger to the Antipodes. The young couple were married in Taunton, and left after a hurried early breakfast for the journey to London.

One of Maria's sisters, be it confessed, stood looking at that disordered breakfast table under the flickering gas-jets, and the heretic stirred in her heart. When all was said and done, wasn't it possible for missions to ask too much of their sons and daughters?

But without regard to all the laws of God and man, that queer bungalow home at Vau Vau proved to be none other than the very door of Heaven. Tropical fruits grew in luscious abundance; a warm sea was at the door—the children played in it, and there were glorious white sands where they could disport themselves.

The early story of Methodist missions in the Friendly Islands about this time reads like an odd page from the days of the Evangelical Revival, but acted in the Garden of Eden. In those far-away palm-fringed islands of the South Seas was the same outpouring of the Spirit, with the same joy, the same burst of song. Chapels sprang up everywhere; a Normal Institution made its appearance; Wesley's Book Room was represented by a printing press at Vau Vau. Canoes, and a smart little frigate served Methodist itineracy. Family prayers were held every night, and the Wesley hymns in a sweet minor key, stole out over those beautiful lagoons and reefs of the sea.

Jabez Bunting in the midst of his own noisy mission conflicts, rejoiced over such a mission field. It was balm to him at the Mission House to get such reports. He loved to hear of the great harvest of souls; it made glorious matter for missionary meetings. Tangible returns mattered much just then. Chapels were raised and given by the island people, under guidance of the singularly devoted missionaries, and the rule of the native king, who was himself a Methodist local preacher. For one such house of worship, the King himself had brought out his ancestral spears and made them into communion rails for the table of the Lord. Once blood-stained battle clubs formed supports for the pulpit in the same house of peace.

Thomas Adams was twice chairman of the Tonga District

and did much valuable work in negotiating peace with heather
chieftains. He translated and printed the Scriptures. Indeed, he
completed the translation of the Bible into the native tongue
edited the whole work, and printed a great part of it with his
own hands, but as the notice in the Minutes of Conference reads
'He so seldom referred to this great achievement that many were
not aware of it.' After all, who was he to boast about the Word
of God? Faithful men had laboured at the translation before
enough for Thomas Adams to find the right word to reach the
heart of Tonga Tabu. The costly pages in that story of great
human endeavour were not for him to linger on, he thought.

About this time the little brown-eyed daughter of the mis
sionary home wrote a letter, and a human document it was. I
read in a breathless manner with very few marks of punctua
tion, as a child tells a story. The small scribe had done the best
she could to improvise a home-made black-edged sheet of paper
Her letter was received by her school-boy brother in England
The father's letters were full of tears and the will of God, but the
child spoke plain fact. A little newcomer had lingered in
their island home; and now he had gone, and Mummy, too
'She had been suffering about three weeks from dysentery
which made her so weak that she had to be lifted about whenever
she wanted to move. On Thursday morning she had a little boy
which lived about an hour, he was named William. She grad
ually became weaker and on Saturday morning we perceived a
great change in her and about eleven o'clock she died. Some
hours after a beautiful smile rose on her countenance.'

Life, this time, had asked too much of Maria French, but she
was through with it now, and could afford to smile. She had had
eight children in thirteen years of married life—far from doctor
and nurses; she had felt the climate a burden through the years
of motherhood. She had been married to a man whose first
interest was in a person's soul, for he never forgot what it had
cost to redeem his own. The body was not so important after
all! When the father there beside the bed baptized the poor

little atom of humanity, he rather wondered why she did not weep over the dying child. But her feet were already feeling for the bottom of Jordan's stream, and life and death were both alike to her. She had given her all.

In time, poor, widowed Thomas Adams returned to England —with a telescope which brother John had given him, a battle club dinted on the heads of enemies before Christ came to Tonga, a Union Jack, a Bible and a troop of little children. Cornwall gave them welcome. Little Alice, not liking the look of things, put up no sort of fight against scarlet-fever, and soon died. Poor Thomas Adams accepted it as the Lord's will, but felt it deeply. One of his sisters came to keep house, and set them up again as comfortably as she could. *It all reads like the story of the Brontës.*

A great story it is, reflecting as in a miniature hung upon the wall of Time, some of the missionary moods, and the miracles that attended in those middle eighteen-hundreds. Maria French and Thomas Adams—man and wife—were moulded of the stuff that made the Kingdom of God real, and helped to establish the Empire besides. Jabez Bunting himself builded better than he knew, with his inexorable maxims for married ministers. It proved a dream that stretched far out beyond Tonga: on the outposts of Christ's Kingdom in Canada, India, China, and Africa, the two sons, the grandson, the granddaughter and great-grandson of Maria French have 'published the Gospel of Peace'!

Dreamers of dreams; we make the taunt with gladness,
Knowing that God, beyond the years we see,
Has wrought the dreams that count with us for madness
Into the texture of the world to be!

Seventeen

'Above All!'

ABOVE tropical Honolulu, the old Punchbowl raises its head, a magnificent mountain top with extinct volcano. On Good Friday, year by year, a great cross is erected in the massive outdoor cathedral on the mountain top. It stands until the sacred days of Easter are over. Strong white searchlights placed on the winding road below, clearly mark out the great out-stretched arms of the cross high up on the mountain, with its exact shadow cast on the low-lying clouds. It is a sight to move the hearts of all those who know well the story of the world's first Easter.

Thousands make their yearly pilgrimage to attend the sunrise service on Easter morning.

The trade winds which blow across the island had made it, at first, difficult to keep the cross erect, and something had to be done to keep the symbol of Love triumphant. It was the children who brought their young hearts and lovely young strength to the task. One of their grown-up leaders shared an inspiration with those children whose parents were born in Korea, Japan, China, America, Portugal, and still other countries. In the task of love, all became one.

For a whole week they worked together gathering stones, and on the day chosen, they formed themselves into a living chain of youth, from their pile to the top of the mountain. From hand to hand they passed the stones, until the huge pile had been transferred to the mountain-top. It was a wonderful task for these whose parents were of so many countries.

Each child of that great company then gave his dime to pay

for skilled labour and bronze and cement, and so the task was completed. The great cross at last stood high and firm upon the ancient mountain-top!

So Easter after Easter now the people of Honolulu climb together to celebrate at sunrise, the triumph of Love Eternal!

Eighteen

'Maoriland's John the Baptist'

IT was the happiest day in Ruatara's life. The sun shone, and the waves lapped upon the beach as they had done before the white man came.

It seemed a long time now, since Ruatara had shipped with two other Maori youths on a whaler. He had been only eighteen at the time, and something had stirred his adventurous heart. For twelve months he had served in Australian and New Zealand waters. It had been a rough life. Who had cared that he was nephew of the great Hongi? Not a soul had even cared, it seemed, whether he lived or died. Hard, hungry days! And his white masters had abruptly discharged him in port of Sydney, without a penny of the money owing to him.

He had then shipped on the whaler *Albion*, but after a few months, had been returned to his own home in the Bay of Islands. In spite of the hardness of the life on ship-board, Ruatara had set his mind on seeing the world, most of all, England and her king, of whom he'd heard such wonderful tales. He shipped on the *Santa Anna*, a sealing boat, as soon as the opportunity came. Surely now he would see the King of England!

Alas, Ruatara's greatest dream had been doomed to disappointment; his first knowledge of the fact that he *was* in England, had been when he found himself ashore, friendless and wretched, ill-treated and cheated of his wages.

In the summer a convict ship left for Australia, and Ruatara was put aboard. Life was wretched, but on board he met one whom he would never forget, the Reverend Samuel Marsden sailing for Ruatara's homeland, New Zealand, in the hope of starting a mission to the Maori people.

Soon after the vessel left port, Marsden noticed among the sailors, this dark-skinned man with a sad face. Pitifully wrapped in an old grey coat, sick and weak, he had a cough, and seemed very near the end of his days. When Marsden learned the story of Ruatara's ill-treatment, he was filled with sympathy and with indignation; immediately he took him under his own care.

With time and treatment, Ruatara gradually recovered. On arrival in Australia his new white friend, Marsden, took him into his own home, whilst he awaited a boat for New Zealand.

At last the captain of a whaling boat agreed to take Ruatara. Alas, time only proved that he had fallen once again into the hands of unscrupulous white men; though the whaler actually came within two miles of Ruatara's home, her captain cared not one jot for the poor fellow's home-sickness, nor his own promise to land him. Later, he put him ashore among strangers on Norfolk Island, having previously defrauded him of his share of the whale oil, valued at about a hundred pounds.

In time, Ruatara somehow managed to get back to Australia; straightway he made for his old friend, Marsden.

When eventually he reached New Zealand, his experiences mounted to a very sorry story of ill treatment. But always, like a thread of light running through was the wonderful kindness that he had received at the hands of one white man. Some day, he suggested to his friends, Samuel Marsden might come to New Zealand; then they would see him for themselves. His friends had not been easily convinced that any white man could be so good a friend.

Soon, Ruatara received from his friend, Marsden, a gift of wheat for seed. No corn had ever waved in Ruatara's young land, and he found himself the centre of a great deal of interest when he committed his precious seed to the soil. After a little while, green ears appeared. Then the ridicule of his friends hurled itself against him; how could such strange green blades yield bread and biscuits like they had eaten on the white man's ships? Some of them actually uprooted his precious stalks to see if there were not something like a potato at the root. Surely Ruatara had been cleverly fooled.

Then came the time of harvest; he threshed out his corn. Unfortunately, poor Ruatara had no mill; he had tried an old coffee-mill, and it had not been a success. His friends laughed at the very idea. A neat little hand-mill from Marsden, eventually arrived by one of the trading boats. Ruatara ground his corn, and made a little cake in an old frying-pan. His friends shouted for joy! *Perhaps, after all, Ruatara had been right!*

Though, by this time, he had assumed his position as chief, with four hundred fighting men under him, Ruatara never again set out on the war-path. He exerted all his powers to get the Sabbath observed on the ships visiting the Bay of Islands.

When at last, his old friend, Marsden, obtained permission to explore the mission field of New Zealand, and sent a letter asking for his help, Ruatara went across to Australia to see what he could do, taking with him four other friendly chiefs.

 ᨁ   ᨁ   ᨁ

Now, at long last, this happiest day of his life had come—Christmas Day, 1814—and his great white friend, Marsden, had held the first Christian service in Ruatara's homeland. Never had he been so happy. He had arranged the seating and the pulpit out of doors, within sound of the sea, and interpreted the message to his people. Yes, Ruatara had never been so happy.

Soon, his friend was writing of this great day: 'A very solemn silence prevailed—the sight was truly impressive. I got up and began the service with singing the Old Hundred Psalm, and felt my very soul melt within me when I viewed my congregation and considered the state we were in. After reading the service . . . it being Christmas Day, I preached from the second chapter of St. Luke's Gospel, the tenth verse: "Behold, I bring you good tidings of great joy". . . . In this manner the Gospel has been introduced into New Zealand, and I fervently pray that the glory of it may never depart from its inhabitants till time shall be no more.'

But it was Ruatara—Maoriland's John the Baptist—who had prepared the way! Only a few weeks after that service, Ruatara died, his work done.

Nineteen

'Shall He Not Hear?'

I WAS lost. I had been to a distant village where there had been a quarrel, and I was on my way home again. Yes, I was lost, as completely as ever I want to be lost.

About the year 1905, one of the volcanoes on the island had come active again. It had poured down its great stream of burning lava, covering everything in its path—trees, shrubs, plantations, and villages, all were covered or swept away. Only one building remained in all that field of black lava—our little L.M.S. Church. For when the lava came to the church, it hesitated; then dividing into two streams, it ran round the church on either side, and on down to the sea. Sometimes one wave flowed over another; sometimes the fresh wave flowed underneath the first and flung it up in a great mountain of broken lava. Then, as the whole field cooled, it cracked, and left thousands of deep fissures running in all directions.

If you could see it to-day, you would see a black barren wilderness of a place, and when you had once crossed it, you would be in no hurry to cross it again—*and I tried to cross it by night!*

I told myself, naturally enough, that I had taken every precaution. The moon was high; I had a strong pressure lamp; and to lead the party I had an old chief who had crossed the lava nearly every day, and knew it as his own hand.

Wise old Samoans advised me against making the journey: 'Don't you go,' they said, 'It isn't safe.' But their good advice fell on deaf ears. I wanted to get back to my work.

All went well with our little party until we came to the lava. Then, within six minutes we were lost. The Samoans tell me there is a clearly-marked track, but even in daylight I had never been able to trace it. Now, in the darkness, the old chief himself was lost. Some of the boys and girls became dissatisfied with the leadership, and slipped away in the darkness by themselves. Then the old chief, angry with himself, began to swing the lantern, so that we could not see where we were treading. Suddenly there was a shout, and I had disappeared.

I had fallen down a crack in the lava rock. I was scratched all over, because it was like falling on jagged pumice, and I was shaken. Slowly and painfully I worked my way up again.

By this time the old man with the lantern had managed to make out a great mountain of lava rock which stood out against the skyline. Only let us reach that, he said, and we would be certain of the way. So, with renewed hope, we started off. We had to walk carefully, but soon it was clear that we were walking on thinly-caked lava which kept giving way under our feet. The old man had lost the way once more.

Now I began to get anxious. I had fallen down a fissure of lava. There were thousands of crevasses like that; supposing another member of our party were to fall; supposing he were to hurt his head and be knocked unconscious. In the darkness spread out all round, he would be left behind all night, perhaps many nights.

I tried as best I could to stop the old man with the lantern, but he was so excited he kept going on. Finally I took hold of him. 'Put the lantern on the ground,' I said. 'Put it down. Now we must get all the party together. This is the first thing. Never mind the track. Let us get together and keep together!'

So we stood and called out across the darkness, telling our party that we would keep calling, and that they must keep answering until every one was found. First one and then another was gathered in.

At last our party was complete. Complete! It was more than complete! For there in the full glare of the lamplight were two small Samoan boys, their white teeth gleaming, and their faces lit up with broad smiles.

'Who may you be?' I asked in surprise, 'and wherever did you come from?'

'We are mountain boys,' they said, 'our father heard you calling in the darkness on the lava. He thought you must be lost, and he sent us down to help.'

They led us back to the track with unerring skill, and never once left us until the lights of the village to which we were going were well in view.

❧   ❧   ❧

Often in this great human world it seems there is nothing to do but to call. Then wonderfully, it is that I hear the echo of the voices of those little hill boys, in some friendly humans who have come to my side: '*Our Father heard you calling through the darkness and He sent us down to help.*'

THE HANDING OVER OF THE BOOKS

[see page 92

Twenty

The Great Hours Strike

*Give all thou canst: high heaven rejects the law
Of nicely calculated less or more.*

Mrs. Ironside sat beaming into the face of her husband. 'Your suggestion? My dear, it's splendid!'

'But I wonder will they accept it?' queried her husband, with puckered brow, 'it's new.'

The excitement that night at Cloudy Bay, had arisen out of the good news that the British and Foreign Bible Society had sent out an edition of five thousand Maori Testaments, four hundred of which were for Cloudy Bay.

For long, the Maoris of the Bay, as elsewhere, had been eager for copies of the precious Book. The earlier parcel of sixteen copies had soon given out. For long months now, Reverend and Mrs. Ironside had been snatching hours from sleep, crouched over their own books, and by the light of candles had been copying out by hand whole epistles for the use of the people. It was laborious.

And now the new copies had come! Four hundred of them! How beautiful they looked! The missionary and his wife had official permission either to sell them, or to give them away. But as Mr. Ironside had toyed with those two possibilities, he had hit upon a happy compromise. 'My dear,' he said, 'let us encourage them in their old custom of a love-gift—*Paremata*.'

The suggestion caught on.

Soon, at the close of a day never to be forgotten, Mr. Ironside was writing by the light of the candles: 'I have often wished I could reproduce the scene in a picture—heaven smiling from

F   81

above; the valley and the surrounding hills clothed in the richest
verdure of early autumn; the crowd of Maoris all with strained
gaze, looking at the distribution; the teacher, as his name was
called out, springing up and rushing to the stand, leaping over
the heads of those who squatted in front of him, clutching the
heap assigned to him, and away back to his place, hugging to his
breast the coveted treasure. An angel in his flight might have
been arrested by the scene.'

But a still greater day was in store. A few weeks later there
was commotion in the air at Cloudy Bay. Wrote Mr. Ironside,
after it was all over, 'All seemed full of repressed excitement;
preparations for a great display were everywhere afoot.... From
the front windows of the Mission House could be seen several
large canoes, fully manned, coming up the bay to the station at
racing speed, each frantically striving to be first. From the back
of the house could be seen a long line of Maoris in Indian file
coming over the saddle in the hills which separated us from the
Sound, each one with a full, heavy basket on his back, and some,
in addition, *with a pig on the string in the hand, guiding him
along*!'

But the climax was not yet. 'While my wife and I were
delighting ourselves looking at the animated scene, listening to
the eager shouting of each fresh arrival, we were told to go inside
the house and shut the door. We were not wanted yet....

'When all was ready we were summoned. There in front of
us was a long heap of baskets, about three feet high, stretching
from one end of the yard to the other. I counted six hundred
baskets, full of potatoes, Indian corn, pumpkins, etc. ... On
the outer side of the heap, tied by the leg to the fence behind,
were seven good-sized pigs. On the heaps of baskets at one
end was a little parcel, tied up in an old handkerchief.

'All being ready, out sprang the master of the ceremonies,
Hoani Koinaki (Johnnie), chief of the Wekenui village in the
Sounds—as fine a specimen of the Maori race as you will see....

'Hoani, tucking up his blanket, with a long native spear in his

and, ran backwards and forwards from one end of the food pile
to the other, striking the baskets at intervals.'

At last he broke the pervading silence, and these were his
memorable words: 'Here is our feast. Take it and give it to our
loving fathers in England; it is all we can do to show our love
to them for their great kindness in sending us the *puka-puka
Holy Book*!'

Then there was a pause. In that little parcel at the end of the
pile—on which we are keeping our eyes—were silver dollars
and crown pieces, English, French, Spanish, American. These
had obviously been in their possession for years. Many of the
coins had been bored through, and used as ear ornaments by the
Maori women. But on this great occasion, all were freely sacri-
ced. Altogether, they mounted up to nine pounds, seventeen
shillings and sixpence! The six hundred baskets and seven pigs
were sold to one of the traders for the sum of twenty-five
pounds! To Mr. Ironside fell the great satisfaction of remitting
to the Bible Society in London, the sum of thirty-four pounds,
seventeen and sixpence—*the first contribution of its kind ever sent
out of New Zealand!*

If the day of distribution had been breathless with joy, the
second had been deeply moving. The happy missionary, as he
took up his journal that night, wrote—and he was almost too
moved to finish his sentence: 'Remembering the sadly degraded
state of these natives a short two years previously. . . .' *Paremata*
—a love-gift! *Truly, when simple hearts are moved, things
begin to happen, thanksgiving becomes a live, practical, joyous
thing!*

Twenty-one

Son of the Wilds

JOOBAITCH often heard his father tell of those unhappy days i the middle of last century, when Australia, in her dire need fo labourers, requested the Home Government to send out convicts The aboriginal owners of what had become the colony's capita Perth, had already begun to dwindle.

Yal'gunga had been the first to greet Captain James Stirling' young representative, as he stepped out of the boat on to Pert territory. He and his family were sitting beside a beautifu spring, when they heard the sound of oars and saw what the thought at first to be a great white spirit returned from the hom of the dead.

Yal'gunga's son, Joobaitch was born during Sir James Sti ling's governorship; and grew up in an atmosphere of kindlines courtesy, and good feeling. He quickly learned to observe th laws of the Great White Spirit. And at the same time his fath taught him their own ancient laws and customs, and he obeye both all his life.

His early years passed among the best of Britain's pioneer Then came white men unlike his friends in high places, chaine and guarded by policemen, and prisoned at night in da sleeping-places. The coming of the convicts and the pensione who were their guards, brought many kinds of evil, includir illnesses hitherto unknown. But Joobaitch was always about tl Government House, loving to be made use of in any way by tl Great White Spirit.

One day, a very desperate convict named Daly escaped fro the road gang and ran far through the bush till he came to tl Darling Range. Policemen and trackers followed, but they r turned without him. Then Joobaitch himself went to the mag rate and asked to be allowed to go alone and bring back Daly.

'But,' said the magistrate, 'you know he is a very big, power-ul man, and a bad one. You could never bring him back by ourself; will you go with the police and help to track him?'

'I think it better I go by myself,' said Joobaitch. 'Daly is in ny country, for the Darling Range is part of our Kangaroo ?otom ground. I will find Daly and bring him back.'

'But Daly is a desperate man.'

'I am not afraid,' said Joobaitch.

He took his club and spear and spear-thrower with him, not s weapons, but to kill his food on the way. Every little hill, ;ully, and waterhole of the ground was familiar to him, and soon le came on Daly's tracks, old tracks at first, then fresh ones. He aw the tracks become crooked as day after day the white man veakened and staggered along. Joobaitch followed slowly but urely, and each day when he caught some food and cooked it he ut on one side a portion for the convict. He found Daly at ast, lying exhausted in a deep gully almost dead from starvation.

He laid down his club and spear and, taking some of the meat le had kept, he put it on his spear-thrower and held it out to Daly, who ate ravenously. Water was near by, as the black man knew, though the white man had not found it. Daly could not walk, but Joobaitch brought him water, and each day hunted for im and fed him, showing him how to make a fire with the black-oy flower stems, and how to cook wallaby, bird, and reptile.

And when Daly's strength came back to him, Joobaitch said, Now we will go back to the Jang'ga—the white men.'

'Not I,' said Daly.

But Joobaitch quietly went on with the day's work, making the fire and cooking the meals, and presently he said again:

'You will come back with me, Daly, because the Great Jang'ga told me you would not be flogged, and they were afraid you would die in these hills, and I told them you would come back.'

The little black fellow was not five feet six, and Daly was a big,

powerful Irishman; but to the astonishment of the whole tow⟨n⟩
ship, Joobaitch walked into the Perth jail one morning with h⟨is⟩
prisoner. With Joobaitch it was always a question of *safety las⟨t.⟩

'Would you like to be Government?' asked the Governo⟨r,⟩
meaning would he like to take some definite office in the State⟨.⟩

There was no question about it. Joobaitch was overjoye⟨d.⟩
He was given some sort of uniform, and the Governor called hi⟨m⟩
and said, 'Some of your people are behaving badly, and I thin⟨k⟩
it is because they do not know the white man's laws. You kee⟨p⟩
your own laws, but you keep ours, too. I appoint you to te⟨ll⟩
your people all about our laws, and how we must punish whi⟨te⟩
or black who breaks them.'

And so it was that when his brother Yaga was shot for th⟨e⟩
murder of white men, Joobaitch and his father kept their grou⟨p⟩
from retaliating. Again, when his betrothed wife was abducte⟨d⟩
and fled back to him for protection, he announced: 'I a⟨m⟩
Government now and cannot kill the abductor.' And becaus⟨e⟩
his people knew him as the best spearman and spear-dodger i⟨n⟩
the south-west, they did not call him a coward. The older amon⟨g⟩
his people listened to him, but the younger ones were spoiled b⟨y⟩
bad white company. One by one they fell ill and died. In th⟨e⟩
end only Joobaitch was left—*the last black fellow of the grou⟨p⟩
that had once owned the Perth area.*

When Bishop Hale arrived in Perth, Joobaitch found a ne⟨w⟩
friend, was baptized, and greatly to his delight, attended th⟨e⟩
same church as the Governor.

Joobaitch was honoured by the whites and loved by his ow⟨n⟩
people. He was over seventy when he died, in 1907, on his ow⟨n⟩
ground, as he had asked to be allowed to do. 'I must die on m⟨y⟩
own ground,' he pleaded, 'where my people have died and gon⟨e⟩
to Koorannup, the home of all our dead, which lies beyond th⟨e⟩
Western Sea.'

So lived, and so passed one of the finest of Australian natives⟨;⟩
when valiant old Joobaitch took that journey to his unknow⟨n⟩
heaven.

Twenty-two

'For Those in Peril . . .'

SOMETHING was amiss. De Angelis, the young navigator confessed himself at a loss to check their whereabouts; the petrol supply was running low; beneath them was a vast expanse of sea, there seemed little left to do now but box the compass, the last resort of the lost.

De Angelis, a dark, wiry young fellow, a Catholic, began to pray; he asked young Johnny Bartek if he was praying. 'No,' was the reply. Johnny had not paid much attention to God or religion, beyond a formal acknowledgment, and now that he was in a jam, he was not going to start calling on God. He would take what was coming to him, and if the end came—well. De Angelis asked Johnny for the little book that he carried—a zipp-edged New Testament, his pastor's farewell gift.

Then the great moment came. The crash proved terrific. They were in the sea now, that a moment or two before had stretched out beneath them. Sergeant Reynolds had remained at his desk till the very last moment, tapping out the S.O.S. that nobody heard.

∞   ∞   ∞

'For me,' says Jim Whittaker, a member of that valiant crew, 'our terrible days on the Pacific represent the greatest adventure a man can have.

'Before the adventure I was an agnostic; an atheist, if you like. But there can be no atheists in rubber rafts, any more than in the fox-holes of Bataan.

'When our Flying Fortress ran out of gas and we prepared
for a crash landing on the sea, Second Lieutenant John De
Angelis, our navigator said, "Do you mind fellows if I pray?"
I recall feeling irritation then. How ashamed I was to remember
that thought in the days to come!

'On our second day in the rubber rafts, I saw Johnny Bartek,
the flight engineer, reading his Testament. None of us kidded
him. Maybe we had a premonition of just how much that little
pocket-Book was to mean to us all.

'On the fourth day Bartek again got out his Testament. Our
three rafts were connected by long ropes, and we pulled them
together for a prayer meeting. We said the Lord's Prayer, and
Colonel Adamson read Bartek's Book. My feeling was that it
wouldn't do any good, but it wouldn't do any harm either.
Captain William T. Cherry, jun., pilot of our plane, then read a
text: "Therefore take no thought, saying: What shall we eat? or
what shall we drink?" I would believe *that*, I said to myself
sceptically, when I *saw* the food and drink!

'By the sixth day it was obvious that we were out of the lanes
of patrol planes and ships, and might never be found. We were
getting weak with hunger.

'That evening I joined passively in the prayers. We all
prayed for food. Then Cherry, who always addressed the Lord
as "Old Master", said, "Old Master, we are in an awful fix, as
You know. We sure are counting on a little something day
after to-morrow, at least. See what You can do for us, Old
Master."

'Cherry then fired off our evening flare in hope that something might happen. It did. The flare's propulsion charge was
faulty and the flaming ball fell among the rafts. We could see
barracuda chasing a school of fish attracted by the glare. In their
efforts to escape, two fair-sized fish leaped into our raft. Each
of us had a small piece of raw fish for breakfast next morning.

'That afternoon I joined more whole-heartedly in the prayer
service. I could now say half the Lord's Prayer without stum-

bling. I shall always remember this particular service—and what followed.

'Cherry prayed: "Old Master, we called on You for food and You delivered. We ask You now for water. If You don't make up your mind to help us pretty soon, I guess that's all there'll be to it. The next move is up to You."

'I think now that Cherry's prayer had everything in it a prayer should have—a petition to God, a resignation to God's will, and an implied belief that the petition will be granted.

'Not long afterwards, I saw a darkening cloud off to our left, from which a bluish curtain descended. It was rain—and moving towards us! "Here she is!" Cherry shouted. "Thanks, Old Master!" In another minute we were deluged by sheets of cold water. We cupped our hands to guide the life-giving rivulets down our throats. After drinking, we filled our mouths and blew the water into our Mae West life-jackets for future use.

'On the ninth day the Lord provided a few bites of food— a little shark about two feet long, which Cherry caught on a bare hook.

'At prayer service on the tenth day, Cherry led the Lord's Prayer and then each man prayed individually. There were open confessions of past sins. I don't mind acknowledging that I made resolutions. And I have kept them. Formerly I couldn't be with any one twenty minutes without an argument; I saw little good in any one, and believed chiefly in Jim Whittaker. Now I accept everyone as being decent and good until he proves himself otherwise.

'Rickenbacker always addressed the Lord as "Our Father". Rick has never professed to be a religious man, but he has the kind of religion that makes this world a better place to live in. One man, when his turn came, prayed that the Lord would let him die and end his suffering. Rick yelled, "Cut that out! Don't bother Him with whining. He answers men's prayers, not that stuff!"

'On our thirteenth day came the first of two miracles that were to cleanse me of agnosticism for ever. The sun was scorching hot. In mid-morning a rain squall appeared, but it passed a quarter of a mile off. For the first time I found myself leading the others in prayer.

'"God," I said, "You know what that water meant to us. The wind has blown it away. It is in Your power to send it back again. It's nothing to You, but it means life to us. Order the wind to blow that rain to us who will die without it!"

'There are some things that can't be explained by natural law. The wind did not change, but the receding curtain of rain began to come slowly towards us, *against* the wind, as though an omnipotent hand were moving it.

'We drank, and caught a store of water. That God-sent rain helped us endure the next four terrible days.

'Of the seven survivors I was the only one whose lower body was not a mass of salt-water ulcers. Our tiny dole of water seemed only to intensify our agonizing thirst. Hunger had weakened us until the slightest effort was exhausting. Our clothing was disintegrating, and the blazing equatorial sun burned us unmercifully. All of us now had touches of delirium. I am sure that only my new-found faith in God sustained me.

'At prayer service on the eighteenth day I prayed as never before—this time for rescue. The end of the service found me with something like my old fortitude. I felt now that help was coming.

'Soon after dawn the next day we saw a plane approaching. We shouted and waved. The plane droned by about three miles without seeing us. If we didn't weep it was only because there wasn't enough moisture in us to form tears.

'On the twentieth morning Cherry cut loose from the rest of us, arguing that if the rafts were spread over a larger area there would be a better chance of one of them being seen. That seemed logical, so I untied my line, too. On my raft were De Angelis and Staff Sergeant Reynolds, who had been our radio-man.

'At dawn on our twenty-first day I was awakened by De Angelis. "Jim," he said, "it may be a mirage, but I think I see something!"

'About twelve miles from us were palm trees! The other two rafts were nowhere in sight. Getting out our aluminium oars, I began what was to be a seven and a half hour pull. During those hours I experienced the second of the divine miracles. What I did in the struggle to reach that island couldn't have been done without divine help.

'My raft-mates were in a pitiable condition. De Angelis spelled me during the row, but was so weak that he could manage only a few minutes at a time. Reynolds lay in the bottom of the raft; his eyes had sunk an inch and a half into his skull, and he resembled a death's-head.

'When we had almost reached the island a perverse current caught us and began to carry us out to sea again. I cried out to God to give me strength, shouting above the rising wind in the fear that He might not hear me.

'Half an hour later it was evident that I was making progress against the current. And then came a new difficulty: a squall that almost blotted the island from our sight. I cried, "God, don't quit me now!"

'He didn't. In the final burst to reach the reef, I was *bending* those aluminum oars against the waves. It was not Jim Whittaker who bent them. I didn't have the strength to bend a pin. I was not conscious of exerting any effort; it was as though the oars worked automatically, and my hands were merely following their motion. There were other hands than mine on those oars.

'To-day, fully recovered, I would hesitate to tackle that stretch of water. Yet, exhausted from three weeks of thirst, hunger and exposure, I accomplished a feat that would have tried a well man!

'We were at the reef now. Carefully we inched the raft across the sharp coral and into the calm water beyond. At two o'clock on that *twenty-first day* we touched the island. We were safe!

'As soon as we were on shore, we knelt down and gave thanks to God.'

❧   ❧   ❧

Johnny Bartek's hard-worn, salt-drenched little New Testament found its way in time, to the office of the American Bible Society. 'Why?' responsible people there asked, 'should those who are set adrift on the trackless seas not be assured of a copy of the New Testament? *What would have happened to Johnny Bartek and his companions if they had not had that little Book?*'

Immediately the Bible House got in touch with the War Shipping Administration in Washington, and offered to place a copy of the New Testament, in a special waterproof container, on every life-raft, and in every life-boat of the merchant service. In a very little time their offer was accepted, priorities secured for the paper, adhesives, lead-foil and cellophane for the envelope.

Then the day arrived for the formal handing over of the first of the twenty thousand. As the two officials from the American Bible Society journeyed down to the docks, one asked, 'What is the name of the ship where we are to have our little ceremony?' He and his companion were stirred to learn that it was none other than the ELIPHALET NOTT—named after the distinguished clergyman, who, with others, came to New York years ago to organize the American Bible Society! Was it coincidence?

In a short time the life-boats of the naval vessels and naval planes were added to the list, later still, the equipment of the great transport vessels. So runs the thrilling sequel! Now because of Johnny Bartek's little New Testament, countless men adrift on the sea may be assured of finding in their outfit, not only flares, fishing-tackle and condensed food, but a little Book that will keep their spirits buoyant and their minds at peace.

Twenty-three

Faith and a Handful of Fish-hooks!

SAMUEL MARSDEN looked up from his work; his face brightened as he made a suggestion that had just occurred to him. 'Why don't you take a trip to New Zealand?' said he to his young English friend, Samuel Leigh, who had found the Australian heat particularly arduous. The truth was, he was sick. The chaplain repeated his suggestion. A change of air would do young Leigh good, and he would also have opportunity of seeing life among the Maoris.

With his eyes full of memories, Marsden was back in that hour, when within sound of the sea, he had preached to the Maoris the first Christian sermon in their land. He knew now that it had been the greatest day of his life. Appropriately enough, it had been Christmas, and he had brought to them the great message of the world's first Christmas: 'Behold, I bring you good tidings of great joy!'

His brig, *The Active*, was now undergoing her last finishing touches at the quay-side. On the morrow she would be ready to sail.

Marsden's young friend was intrigued with his suggestion; he liked the idea that he should set foot on another strange shore—especially one over which the explorers had written the one word: 'Dangerous!' Imagination could hardly conjure up what that might mean.

Yes, he would go.

ʅﻬ   ﻬ   ﻬ

Though Marsden had warned him of much that he might see, he was utterly unprepared for the first sight that met his eyes as

93

the boat drew in—a gruesome row of tattooed Maori heads, exhibited for sale. It shook him. Nor was that all; with the passing of days and nights, he was called upon to be the spectator of many other revolting practices. The horrors of a cannibal feast shook him still further: 'God! God!' he cried, 'What can I do?'

That was the cry that was never to leave him. Across the waters which separated this strange, barbarous New Zealand from his own England, there rang now in his ears the words of a great leader: 'Go not only to those who need you, but to those who need you most.' He himself had been but a small child when that great man, Wesley, had been carried to his grave by six poor men.

So the young Englishman, Leigh, came, saw things he would never forget, left—and in time, came again.

In the interval of three years he had accomplished much; he visited London to storm the leaders at the Mission House with the needs of these Maori people. From overburdened shoulders, however, he was to receive little practical help. The heads of the Mission had already as much as they could manage.

Undaunted, he set out on an intensive campaign up and down the country, gathering from all sorts of people all sorts of gifts— dress-fabrics, hardware, jewellery, fish-hooks, and a dozen other things. At last, to the amazement of many, he had gathered in kind, enough to enable him to commence his mission to the Maoris.

He had also found in his native Staffordshire a gentle young lady who would be his helpmeet.

So they came, the Reverend Samuel Leigh, and his wife, with her stout heart, her dainty full-bodiced frocks and her fears—to a little land at the end of the earth.

Summer was well advanced when they landed at the Bay of Islands, in the northern part of New Zealand. The heat quivered over the strange, new coastline.

At first there was no place where Mrs. Leigh could unpack her own precious household things. For months the newcomers were housed with their friends of the Anglican Mission at Paihia.

The young husband was busy with a hundred interests, poring over his books, setting his hands to all manner of practical tasks, making diligent use of every opportunity that offered itself. So much there was to do! If only the summer days could be twice as long! If only he might hurry! Some things there were, seemingly, that could not be done in a hurry.

It was a Sunday in August, over six months later, before he was able so much as to preach to the people in their own language. How proud of him was Mrs. Leigh that day. He, too, was proud, that day.

Eager now to find a suitable place for his mission, he waved Mrs. Leigh his affectionate farewell one early morning, and set off with five natives in a boat. In no time, he and his boys were being blown out to sea. A tremendous storm raged. When next they were able to guide their tiny craft towards land, they found themselves, to their surprise, well into the harbour at Whangaroa. The natives in these parts were all too well known for their ferocious cannibalism.

The approach of the little storm-blown boat immediately brought an angry crowd down to the beach, uttering blood-curdling yells and threats. It was certainly a critical moment. Then greatly daring, the young missionary stepped out with the cry: 'Stand back! I have fish-hooks!' And from his pocket he threw over their heads a handful of hooks—a device of less than a split second's thought, which saved the situation. While the blood-thirsty, half-clad warriors, like so many children, were busy scrambling for the fish-hooks, Leigh lost no time in making his way back to the boat and his friendly Maori boys who were to take him back safely to the Bay of Islands.

❧   ❧   ❧

Scarcely had a year passed, and the young missionary was
drawing near to that same shore. In the meantime, it had been
settled upon as the most likely place for the establishment of the
headquarters of the Mission. *Safety?* That was his *last* thought.
Leigh might very well have stepped ashore with secret fears as
he left the *St. Michael*. Incredible as it seemed, those fears were
quickly dispersed by the cries of the Maoris: '*Haeremai!*
*Haeremai!—Welcome, welcome! This is the white man who gave
us fish-hooks!*'

And thus dramatically, the Methodist Mission found its birth-
place in New Zealand, to be threatened again and again, but to
win in the end, a deep and lasting place in the affection of the
great Maori people.

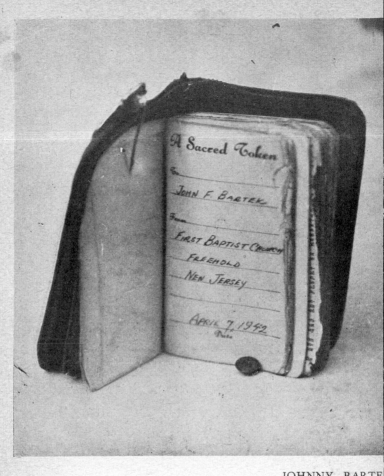

A Sacred Token

For
JOHN F. BARTEK

From
FIRST BAPTIST CHURCH
FREEHOLD
NEW JERSEY

APRIL 7, 1942
Date

JOHNNY BARTE

NEW · TESTAMENT

[*see page 92*]

Twenty-four

'Sursum Corda!'

MISSIONARY GOLDIE was worried. Old Kere stood before
him with sixty pounds. It seemed a far call to those
earliest days when the old man had done everything in his power
to hinder.

Now he stood before the missionary with the total product of
his year's work. It was Thanksgiving time, and this was Kere's
offering.

'But Kere, you cannot afford to give like this,' remonstrated
the missionary. Old Kere did not answer for a moment or two;
his heart was very full. Then he said: 'When I look at those boys
of mine I cannot afford *not* to give.'

৹   ৹   ৹

Milton, Kere's eldest of six, was reckoned one of the best
boys of the Mission school. When the Mission had installed the
first wireless telephone transmitting service in the Western
Pacific, it was Milton who served as operator.

With the years, further chances of service came to Milton.
The Government Medical Superintendent arrived in the Solomons to look into the leper question for the Colonial Government. He approached Mr. Goldie at the Mission headquarters.

'Can you lend us a boy to go round with us?' he asked.

'Yes,' said Mr. Goldie, happily, 'you can have Milton.'

The important task was done, and Mr. Goldie and the Medical
Superintendent met once more.

'Well, how did you get on with Milton?' asked the missionary.

'Fine!' answered the doctor, 'we never had the work done
better.'

As for Milton, when he was able to talk over his experiences quietly, he had something to say about the doctor. 'Every morning,' he said, impressively, 'when I went up into the bow of the boat to kneel at my prayers, the Doctor came and knelt beside me there!'

∾ ∾ ∾

Yes, truly, Old Kere who stood before the missionary, had cause for thanksgiving! Besides Milton, his youngest son—John Wesley Kere—was a boy to make his old father proud! When the British Solomon Island Government sought to bestow the Coronation Medal for scholastic attainment, it was John Wesley Kere who received it. Proudly that medal was placed on the wall of the Mission College!

Old Kere's youngest lad was soon off to Fiji to attend the medical school. As the months went by, news reached his old father of the worthy place he was winning for himself in the studies of the school, in the cricket eleven, and as captain of the Rugby team. It was all cause for thanksgiving!

And how warmly old Kere's heart would have been moved could he have lived to know that in 1941, John Wesley Kere, his son, would win the British Medical Association's Gold Medal for surgery in the Pacific!

Twenty-five

'Not by their Size'

Not by their size
Measure we men
Or things. . . .

WOULD the child live? A dark cloud hung over the modest Scottish home. It seemed that the hopes quickened by the birth of a son, were to be blasted. The doctor was not hopeful; life was hanging by the slenderest thread. The young parents pleaded with their God that the little life might be saved; they made a vow that if he were spared, they would dedicate him to service among the heathen. Days passed. The little fellow rallied.

Among friends and neighbours he became affectionately known as 'Little Johnny Geddie'; he remained known by this same for the rest of his life—and what a life!

Driven from the Old Land by economic pressure when Johnny was still a lad, his parents did what they could to found a home in the new country of Nova Scotia. There the Scottish clock-maker and his wife and child found themselves part of a little hard-working, rugged community.

In time, prosperity brought into their midst many forms of evil—drunkeness was widespread; moral laxity followed, and much sadness crept into the life of the people. Little Johnny Geddie was fortunate in having a good home, and a good school. Whilst many lads were wasting their time, he was revelling in his tales of the South Seas. Captain Cook had just fired the imagination of the world by discovering a group of some thirty odd islands in the romantic South Seas. He called them by the

99

beautiful name, New Hebrides, after the Scottish Hebrides. They bore some similarity in appearance.

To Little Johnny Geddie, the youth reading his story in Nova Scotia, Captain Cook's discovery sounded very romantic, and very far off.

One day news of a tragic happening in those lovely islands reached Johnny Geddie's simple home. John Williams had fallen a martyr to the faith. It was sad telling. People said that the work must not stop; a successor must be found.

Johnny Geddie was by this time a young minister of the Church. All that he had ever read and thought about the South Seas rushed back into his mind and heart with a new urgency. Perhaps the South Seas were not so far off after all, if one's duty lay there. He was still small of stature, and he was retiring of manner, with a voice as gentle as that of a woman. At first glance, he seemed to have none of the qualities a man should have who would follow in the steps of a martyred missionary, but one forgot the smallness of figure, remembering only a great spirit.

After much humble deliberation, he came to the point where his mind was clear on the issue; and with that decision he led his Church out into a new work. We honour the pioneer; we bear in lasting memory the man who cuts the first path into hitherto inaccessible lands, and this Little Johnny Geddie did. He brought to his beloved Presbyterian Church of Nova Scotia the honour of *being the first Church in an overseas Dominion to send a missionary to heathen lands*. It was both a tiny, and a poor Church, whose members wrested a living from the young country's unbroken forests.

This great missionary adventure began in a little boat of some hundred and ninety-seven tons, and a hazardous trip it proved to be! Ice formed on the harbour the night before Little Johnny Geddie and his young wife were to sail, and completely held up the departure of the vessel.

In time, the weather improved; the familiar shores were soon lost to sight. It was no easy thing to leave the homeland they knew. Terrific storms buffeted the little vessel; it sprang a leak, and the men had almost constantly to be at the pumps. Fresh provisions gave out.

Never was any cluster of stars more welcome than when the beautiful Southern Cross appeared, heralding the end of their days in the tiny ship.

The young missionary couple chose the island of Aneityum, with its fine harbour, as their base. The dark-skinned, curly-headed natives, they soon discovered, were savage in the extreme. War was part of their accepted scheme, life was of no value, blood flowed every day. A man was seldom if ever seen without his club and spear; women lived in bondage of body and mind, brutality their earthly lot. The tribal practice of strangling widows to accompany their dead husbands into the spirit world was common; eleven widows were thus strangled near their home in the very first year the young missionary and his wife spent on the island. Their own simple property was threatened by fire, but they were not the sort of people to know defeat in so short a time—and they had come so far.

The language of the people had never been reduced to writing, and this was one of the early tasks. The people, however, were not willing to part with their words to a stranger; but that could not spell defeat to Little Johnny Geddie; he hit upon a plan. He went around with a pocketful of biscuits, and bartered them for the strange sounds he heard. In this ingenious way, he gathered at the end of a long time of patient trying, enough words to make an alphabet of twenty-one letters.

He opened schools, but the island people refused to send him scholars, unless he undertook to pay the parents for allowing them to come. It was a long, uphill task.

In time, better understanding was developed. They came to trust this strange little white man and his wife. Of course the very fact that he was a white man stood in his way—the sandal-wood gatherers were also white men. The memory of a das-tardly act was still all too fresh. Three sandalwood vessels had anchored in one of their beautiful bays. The crews, on coming ashore, had quarrelled with the natives and used firearms against them. About thirty of the poor, terrified islanders, including men, women and children, took shelter in a cave near at hand. The white sailors then perpetrated a dastardly act for which it was hardly likely the island people would soon forgive them; they tracked the natives to the mouth of the cave, piled up brushwood, and set fire to it. In a short time the whole company within the smoke-filled cave were silenced in death. Masters of the situation, the villainous newcomers then supplied themselves abundantly with wood, yams, and eggs, and departed at will.

Little wonder suspicion held up the good work of the white missionary! On one island, at least, was a standing rule that a white man should be murdered at sight. Words are poor things to convey an idea of the magnitude of the task that faced these two lone souls, John Geddie and his wife.

In time, twenty-five white schools were sprinkled throughout the land. The indomitable little missionary prepared and printed a book of twelve pages; hymns were struck off on his tiny press. The island people were encouraged to come to the Mission home, as well as to church.

Translations of the Gospels, the New Testament, and finally the whole Bible followed in time. As the people slowly progressed in Christian things their missionary proposed to them— these erstwhile savages—that they should put aside some part of their arrowroot crop to pay for their books. This was done— and done so whole-heartedly, that they paid for the whole of the printing of the New Testament in their own language. A far step from the suspicion with which they had bartered the very sounds of their language for biscuits!

In time, fine native Christians gathered to help in the work. At the close of eleven years the entire population of three thousand, five hundred people on Aneityum were under instruction, and two thousand of them were daily readers of the Scriptures! God had not forgotten the vow of those two simple souls beside the cot of their little one. When their son, grown of years, passed on, there was erected in the largest church on that far-away island, a plaque bearing these triumphant words:

> WHEN HE LANDED IN 1848 THERE
> WERE NO CHRISTIANS HERE, AND
> WHEN HE LEFT IN 1872 THERE WERE
> NO HEATHEN

Twenty-six

'Warrior Brown'

'THUD!' What was that? A potato had hit 'Warrior Brown' a nasty blow. Now in the old days, as everybody knew, that would have been a dangerous thing to do. It would certainly have meant a fight, if not worse. But now, all eyes upon her, 'Warrior' calmly picked up the potato, and without a word, put it in her pocket.

'Warrior Brown' had changed her evil ways. The Maoris passed the word around. It was weeks since she had been drunk, and her temper had not flared of late. People and dogs, alike, had got out of her way when her temper had flamed. The truth was, something had happened to 'Warrior Brown'. She had until now, well earned the nickname in her readiness to fight. A little pioneer group of Salvation Army folk had come, and listening to them, 'Warrior' had become a Christian. She was 'Warrior Brown' now in the army of Jesus Christ.

This night she was speaking in the open air, telling of the change that had come into her life. It was rather an unruly meeting. While she was speaking, some person on the edge of the crowd began throwing things at the speakers.

Months went by, and then the Harvest Thanksgiving came; people assembled, bringing their gifts. Along came 'Warrior' with her offering—a little bag of potatoes. How the people stared! What an unexpected witness! The old Maori woman then quietly explained that she had taken home the insulting potato on the former occasion, and had cut it up into pieces with an 'eye' on each, and had planted them all. *She was now presenting in 'Thanksgiving' the increase that had followed on her Christian*

way of retaliation, as further evidence of the change in her life.
Who would ever forget that Harvest Thanksgiving day?
'Warrior Brown' had demonstrated a miracle of love!

Twenty-seven

'One of our Planes is Missing'

THE planes had been overhead all morning. The Solomon Island boys watched them with interest and awe, and heard the deafening noise they made. The Americans had arrived.

The boys knew little of the actual mechanism of planes, but they did know that men were in danger out there beyond the reef. One of those roaring monsters from above the coconut palms had fallen into the sea.

In time they managed to reach the two young airmen. One of them was badly wounded. Skilfully and gently they got him into the canoe, and made their way to the village.

They knew that by far the worst part of the journey lay before them. They prepared a big canoe for the hazardous trip along the coast to where, forty miles away, they would find a native medical practitioner who had both wireless transmitter and medical equipment. But they did not speak their thoughts.

The two American boys were filled with apprehension; brave to face the dangers of combat, they felt now less safe than they had done in their plane.

'Where are you taking us?' one of them asked.

'Down the coast to the native doctor,' they answered him.

'The native doctor!' the young pilot ejaculated. The answer conjured up in his mind only the dark practices of witchcraft.

'Where have we dropped?' he ventured, finding in mere speech some relief. One in the moving swiftly canoe answered, 'On Santa Ysabel.'

Dead silence.

Then the one question tormenting the young pilot and his

sick friend came out: 'Is that where they cook and eat white people?'

At that, the native boys forgot their paddling for a moment, and laughter rocked the boat from end to end: 'No! No!' they exclaimed, 'We are all Christians!'

Gone was the tension.

On and on raced the great canoe with its precious burden to a beach below the native doctor's hut. Between them they carried the young wounded airman up the hill. Food had to be carried up also, and water to be sterilized before the wounds of the sick man could be tended. The native boys moved swiftly and gently about their self-appointed tasks. They kept a careful watch, never relaxing for so much as a moment by day or by night.

On the third day a boat arrived from the young airmen's headquarters on another island. As they took their departure, they shook hands with their new friends, lost for words in which to express their thanks. The native lads—Good Samaritans of the Pacific—lined up on the beach.

Officials present at headquarters, when the young pilot arrived to give his report, would never forget how his face lit up when he said: 'Sir, you should have seen their expressions when they said, "We are all Christians here!" Shure,' he added, 'they were Christians, all right!'

∾·   ∾·   ∾·

Later, the airman learned that behind the boys' wonderful Christian spirit lay twenty odd years of devotion of a missionary woman, Mrs. Emily Sprott.[1]

[1] Mrs. Emily Sprott, M.B.E., for years a Melanesian Mission worker on Ysabel Island in the Northern Solomons, was for thirteen months the only white woman there, and when the Japanese were in occupation, lived in the jungle, moving constantly to avoid capture.

The Transformed Isle

CUPID is an important factor in South Sea stories. On the twenty-third of December, 1787, a small ship left England under orders to proceed to the Society Islands for the purpose of procuring plants of the bread-fruit-tree. Certain islands of the West Indies had been discovered without natural food supply, and it was believed that if trees of the bread-fruit were transplanted, these islands would become habitable.

So King George consented to the sending out of the little *Bounty*. Her 'burthen was nearly two hundred and fifty tons'. She carried officers and crew numbering forty-four, and two men skilled in the culture of trees. She was to sail as expeditiously as possible round Cape Horn. 'The ship was stored and victualled for eighteen months.'

After lengthy delay, through contrary winds and bad weather, the little *Bounty* sailed from Spithead just before Christmas, reaching Tahiti in October of the following year, having sailed twenty thousand and eighty-six miles.

Could those men of England have foreseen the results of the voyage, it is doubtful whether even the stoutest heart among them would have embarked on an undertaking fraught with so much tragedy.

Soon they were about the task for which the voyage was made. For nearly six months they collected and stowed away the young trees. The sailors, however, were a good deal more interested in the dusky girls than in the young trees. So as the cargo began to grow, and the time for leaving their sweethearts drew nearer, they conceived a bold plan. 'For twenty-three weeks,' Captain Bligh wrote, 'we had been treated with the utmost affection and

regard, which seemed to increase in proportion to our stay.'
The men in the fo'c'sle would have told the same story. But
they had to leave.

The actual leaving came more suddenly than was expected, a
violent storm threatening. They called at an island to take on
water, fruits, goats and other live stock. On the twenty-sixth of
April the *Bounty* put out to sea.

During the stay, their doctor had died through indolence and
intemperance, but the captain felt satisfied that the ship was in
good trim, the crew in perfect health, the trees flourishing.

Then suddenly, or so it seemed—just before sunrise on the
unforgettable April the twenty-eighth, mutiny broke out. It
seemed that the chief cause was the desire of the sailors to return
to the Tahitian women; though the state of affairs was perhaps,
aggravated by the stern rule of the captain.

Just before sunrise, while Captain Bligh was yet asleep,
Fletcher Christian with the master-at-arms, gunner's mate and a
seaman, broke into his cabin. Waking him, they quickly seized
his arms and bound them behind him, threatening him with
instant death if he spoke or made the least noise. The captain
called wildly, in spite of their threats, but it was useless. Three
men stood at his cabin door, besides the four who struggled
within, with a cutlass and muskets and bayonets. He was hauled
out on to deck in his shirt, suffering great pain from the tightness
with which they had bound his hands. He who had given orders,
was now humiliated in the reception of them. 'Hold your
tongue, sir, or you are dead this minute!' was shouted at him.

It was all over in minutes; the officers were called on deck, a
small boat was launched to receive the unfortunate Bligh and
those who were to share his fate. The boat was so small that the
eighteen men and the Captain had all they could do to cram into
her. The remaining crew on the little *Bounty* tossed in a few
stores, and cut them adrift: a hundred and fifty pounds of bread,
sixteen pieces of pork, six quarts of rum, six bottles of wine, and
twenty-eight gallons of water.

Stark necessity brought to the fore all their powers of endurance. They rationed the supplies at a minimum that would sustain life and give energy to their arms. And they set out to row three thousand six hundred miles!

At night they spread their coverings to the dew, and sucked them to save water. They caught a few sea-birds to vary their monotonous diet. They suffered unbelievable hardships. At long last they landed at an island, thence they shipped home to England, arriving there just on three years after they had set out.

An expedition was dispatched to search for the mutineers who had so wilfully defied authority. Fourteen of them were captured (eight having joined Fletcher Christian on the *Bounty*, two having lost their lives on Tahiti). These poor creatures were clapped into irons; four died in a shipwreck on the way home. Of the ten remaining, 'four were acquitted; one was discharged on account of an informality in the indictment; the other five were found guilty and were condemned to death. Of these, two received pardon, and the three others were executed at Spithead,' from which place they had shipped four years before.

But the mutineers had not remained where they could be easily captured. As soon as they had cut Bligh and his companions adrift, Fletcher Christian assumed command of the *Bounty*, and made back to Tahiti. But this seemed too dangerous a place in which to stay, little as they ever expected the crew of the open boat to reach England.

Leaving at Tahiti those who wished to remain behind, Fletcher Christian and his shipmates left, taking with them six native men, ten women and a girl of fifteen, and sailed away to an island called Pitcairn.

The island, though small—five miles in circumference, and scarcely more than two miles across at its widest point—was covered with a luxuriant growth of trees. It did not take long to discover that the island had been, and was probably still inhabited. Traces of former human habitation were found. As day followed day and no one molested them, the mutineers began to feel more secure, and preparations were made for a permanent settlement. During the earliest days on Pitcairn, the fugitives spent their time in caves and tents whilst their dwellings were being erected.

All traces of the *Bounty* were destroyed by fire, after everything that might be of value was removed. Thus their last link with civilization was broken.

Then there ensued what has been called 'a hell on earth'. How could it be otherwise? Men were constantly weighed down with guilt and self-accusing. The first trouble began when one of the mutineers named Williams lost his wife, and wanted to take another. There hung over all a dreadful pall of treachery, oppression, and bloodshed. One of the sailors who had been brought up in a distillery in Scotland, discovered a way to distil alcohol from the roots of a native plant. Thus drunkenness was added to many other vices.

Before long all the native men were dead, and all the white men but one. That one was John Adams. Picture him, if you will, the forlorn monarch of a helpless people, shut up on an island of the Pacific with a company of native women, a number of children, and his own bitter memories.

Consider then, this amazing thing which happened. In a sailor's trunk, Adams discovered two books. One was a Bible. As he pored over its pages, there was awakened within him a sense of his reponsibility for the young generation around him who had been served such a bad start. He repented of his sins, and began to live a God-fearing life. It was a late beginning, but he engaged in the gigantic undertaking with all his heart. Twenty-three children had been born to the mutineers. John Adams set about the work of teaching those children, with earnestness, aided solely by the great Book. It was a remarkable undertaking.

In time, John Adams had the satisfaction of seeing the children of such parentage, growing up law-abiding, happy, peaceable, industrious folk, with a love of virtue and a quickened sense of morality. Years passed. The community prospered. The children grew and married, and more children were born. A beautiful feature of the transformed isle was the love that united them as one family under the fatherly care of John Adams.

Then one day, nearly twenty years later, a ship from America called at the island by chance, and brought back the first news to the world that had all but forgotten the mutineers who had escaped the hangman in 1790. John Adams reigned in peace, king, preacher, and teacher of the little community. He hoped that only ships from America would visit him, for he had no hankering for the gallows of England. But England had given up bothering about him, and he lived and died in peace.

The captain of the visiting American vessel, the *Topaz* had written: 'I think them a very humane and hospitable people; and whatever may have been the errors or crimes of Adams, the mutineer, in times back, he is at present a worthy man, and may be useful to navigators who traverse this immense ocean.'

And the secret? A Book.

The island was one hundred per cent Christian. Nowhere on earth was life more safe.

DANIEL BULA

[see page 183

Twenty-nine

'Where Men make an end of Mating'

THE *Rangitane's* passengers had gone off to their cabins, tired but well satisfied that they had had a good day. It had been an ideal day for deck life—tennis, quoits, ping-pong, and many had brought out their knitting and books.

Before they could assemble on deck again, they would be themselves part of an epic story, for early on the fateful morning of the twenty-seventh of November, 1940, they were to be awakened by something that sounded like gun-fire. But it was only three-fifty a.m., and they were only yet thirty-six hours out of port!

The soft moments ticked by; the noise had not been very loud nor very alarming. A number of the nervous ones had begun dressing, which seemed a stupid thing to do at that hour of the morning.

Then, in less than a minute, a salvo of shells hit the side of the ship! Their entire floating world staggered beneath them; the air was full of terror and din—smashing cabins and crashing glass. A piercing cry from an injured woman rent the darkness.

Somehow, the passengers mechanically remembered the instructions they had been given at boat-drill. It all seemed unreal. Many were stunned by flying debris. Lunging forward through smoke and darkness, seeking one of the exits to the upper deck, a number discovered it blocked by a raging furnace. In a few minutes that seemed hours, they made their way out through another exit. Dawn was just breaking—cold and with a steady drizzling rain falling, and a heavy swell running. A black-looking ship lay at anchor about two hundred yards off. Beside her were two other sinister-looking ships, one flying the

German flag, both of them showing on their bows the Japanese colours.

Already some of the wounded had been brought up from the blazing cabins. One of them, badly wounded, died there on deck. The lifeboats were got away as they were filled. But what were they to do? And where were they to go? Others of the wounded passengers died in the boats as they were being rowed round and round waiting for orders. There was no panic, the passengers and crew behaved as in a dream.

On the brightly lighted bridge of their ship, that a few hours earlier had been their happy world, they could now pick out the figure of a German sailor in white uniform, as he signalled to the raider. The searchlights were full on the unfortunate ship.

It was soon clear to those in the lifeboats that they were meant to draw in alongside the black ship which stood near. Wearing only the scantiest of clothing, shoeless and hatless, and in many cases, wounded, the women passengers along with the men were soon clambering up the rope-ladder at the side of the vessel. It was like a nightmare at that hour of the morning.

With uncanny precision they were being marshalled below. Life on the Pacific raider had begun. Men and women were separated, both parties cramped for space; water was strictly rationed, food offered was bad, and hygienic provisions almost nil. There was no possibility of seeing their whereabouts when daylight was fully come; they were shut down below sea-level.

At night many lay wakeful, listening to the tramp, tramp, tramp of the guard overhead, and the miserably monotonous swirl of the water against the ship's side. At intervals, a tiny pocket torch was focused through a small grating high up in the wall, and a face peered through at the uncomfortable prisoners below.

Morning came, and night! Nobody spoke of the misery of the hours of darkness. An officer came in now and then to ask further questions. The doctor entered to say that one of their number, a young woman of twenty-two, had died on board.

Next they were being guided up on deck for a solemn service, as her body was confided to the great ocean. The German crew stood at attention on the deck, the Captain made a speech, a Church of England chaplain, a fellow-prisoner, said a few words and offered a prayer. All had been deeply moved by the young woman's courage. The Nazi salute split the air, and it was over.

After a further time of confinement, a small ship bearing a Japanese name and flying the Japanese flag, became temporary home to a number of the prisoners. Conditions were more bearable. There was still an appalling lack of water; the only food served was nauseating, unchanging from day to day, much of it unfit for human consumption. Other prisoners were added from time to time, women and children among them.

As the routine came to be known, any further signs of raiding activity grew to be recognized. Besides being kept under closer guard, this often meant the coming of more prisoners. As each fresh batch came below, the early-comers pressed round for news. What was happening was something everybody wanted to know. What was to happen to them? That, alas, was something that nobody could know.

The days and nights were now becoming insufferably hot, the space more and more cramped. Added to this, was their running into the monsoon. For three days and three nights the miserable little ship buffeted her way forward only by straining and creaking, hardly able to keep up with her raider escorts. The terrific noise and discomfort below, especially for the sick and wounded, may best be left to the imagination. All were wonderfully courageous; odd little jokes were passed from one to another. One morning, those below awakened to the smell of fire and the sight of the ship's firemen tearing down charred, smoking woodwork. Over-crowded, and in a shark-infested sea, the realization that the lifeboats were woefully insufficient, added nothing to calm of mind.

Then things not hitherto part of the routine began to happen. Anchor was dropped by each of the boats; the Commander came aboard. Hours that afternoon were spent in making the wounded comfortable—limbs were X-rayed and reset. Then the ships parted once more.

Life was becoming hotter and dirtier and more sordid. But, as all through, folk managed to keep up their spirits. Grizzly beards appeared. Some of the women made odd-looking garments from the few sheets issued. A curious bag of spoils made its appearance, blouses, shoes, and of all things, a parcel of flaxen wigs.

Then after nearly four weeks of confinement and semi-starvation, the prisoners suddenly came to the realization that they were being put ashore.

Emirau or Squally Island proved to be their landing spot. The island itself, they discovered, was somewhat flat, irregular in shape, about twelve miles long and six in width. But wonderful it seemed to set foot firmly on shore!

On the island were the manager of a plantation and his wife, with whom the castaways made an early acquaintance. Another white family lived a few miles away. When the prisoners had been landed, a promise had been extracted that no attempt would be made to summon help for forty-eight hours. The raiders threatened a reprisal bombing attack on the island if, for any reason, the undertaking were disregarded.

As far as the raiders knew, the four hundred and ninety-five castaways were without communication with the outside world, save for a lifeboat and oars, and a small quantity of oil. There was no running water on the island, only what could be gathered from the rains. Nine head of cattle—all that the little island possessed—had already been carried off by the raiders, save for one unruly member of the herd that escaped into the swamp. It served later to feed the castaways. Some weevil-eaten rice was also left by the raiders.

᭡   ᭡   ᭡

Various adventures on the island will be retold in days to

come; I must be satisfied to tell here the experiences of one couple. Judge Stuart and Mrs. Stuart—a niece of the famous Dr. Starr Jameson of the South Africa raid—had left the Friendly Islands for a new appointment in British Guiana, little dreaming that an adventure of this kind lay in store for them.

After a few hours ashore, they decided to find their way to the native village some distance off to see what the prospects were of obtaining food or other relief. The native village lay to the windward, about ten miles away. The natives were of dangerous cannibal stock.

Though warned of the danger they ran, the two of them set off, looking like story-book castaways, making their way by small paths through the jungle. Counting a good deal on what they knew of the influence of missionaries on people of the South Seas, they pushed on, weak and faint, making their way slowly and cautiously in case of alarming any they might meet unaccustomed to strange white people.

They came, in time, to the picturesque village hidden within dense, tropical vegetation. The village was quiet. A little herd boy seemed the only inhabitant. A scanty knowledge of certain native dialects of the South Seas enabled the newcomers to make known to the child that they wanted to see the chief. Without rising, he pointed to the largest of the huts. As they drew near, to their surprise, they heard voices singing:

> *Jesus loves me, this I know,*
> *For the Bible tells me so....*

A fine, tall Solomon Islander was conducting a simple service of worship. The hut proved to be the newly-built native church. They bowed as they made their entrance, and sat for a time listening.

How reassuring, after the brutalities suffered at the hands of their white-skinned and supposedly civilized captors!

As daylight lessened, they withdrew and returned to the little copra hut they had taken over as sleeping quarters. What seemed like hours passed. They lay in an uneasy sleep on the raised floor of the hut.

The Judge suddenly roused his wife, 'Sit up! Natives coming!' Their hearts all but stood still. Then in the dim light they saw a pair of black out-stretched hands offering them a pannikin of water. With the gift of water was also a tray of smoking-hot sweet potatoes. The voice said the word for food, '*Kai Kai*'— and it proved to be that of the Solomon Islander. They accepted his simple offering, and when they had appeased their hunger and thirst, somewhat, made as though to set aside some of the gift for to-morrow.

'Why no eat?' was the surprised question of their new friend.

'We want to keep it till to-morrow.'

'More to-morrow,' they were told.

         ❦   ❦   ❦

When the new day was come, the two castaways made their way into the village to talk with this friendly black missionary. In conversation he said, 'Me tell you my story, yes?'

They learned that he was the son of cannibal parents of the Solomon Islands. Coming under the influence of missionaries he had become Christian, and had been sent to be educated as a catechumen. His training behind him, he had managed to get to Emirau, where till then, no missionary had settled among the people. Many of them had become Christian and had been baptized.

'I t'ink none cannibal now,' he said, simply, 'I t'ink all friendly. I tell you my story. I sing to you, yes? He took up his guitar, twanged the strings and sang tunefully.

Next day was Christmas Day! It proved for the castaways a remarkable Christmas Day. Just on dawn, the Judge and his wife were awakened by some of their island friends bearing to them Christmas gifts—three eggs and a small water-melon—all they had. *How rich their giving!*

❧   ❧   ❧

The raiders had departed, believing that they had destroyed the only means of communication with the outside world, save the boat and oars they had left. They could not know that hidden away up a tidal creek, lay a small launch belonging to the missionary. Soon the launch was putting off for a distant island where a message could be sent to the outside world.

In time a rescue ship was on its way to take off the castaways.

As Judge Stuart and his wife took leave of their new friends, they suggested that now that they were going back to the white man's country, they would see what they could do about repaying them. But the island people shook their heads: 'We give you. You give us? No,' they said. 'We are Christians; we give you because you have so little.'

So did two castaways find the spirit of the world's first Christmas on a little island in the Pacific. Here, in the midst of war, was a place where men had made an end of hating.

Thirty

'Young, Strong and Free'

CHEERS, cheers, a thunder of cheers rose from the great crowd of Suva's football enthusiasts. Isikeli had scored again. He was their best player; still, they had hardly expected three splendid goals against the crack Tongan team in the Test Match.

Few did not know Isikeli, a young teacher of the Mission, a very likeable young man, a chief and scout-master. He had won immense popularity with the Europeans as well as with his own people. Some of his Mission friends remembered, with a thrill, that his name derived from the Biblical name, Ezekiel, meaning 'strong'. Isikeli was strong, they agreed, he was the strength of their team. His play as wing three-quarter had been the outstanding event of Fiji's sport during the year.[1] Yes, Isikeli was strong!

❧   ❧   ❧

Time passed, and a great Scout rally was due. Weeks and weeks had been filled with preparations.

Scouts gathered from far and near; anticipation ran high. The Saturday morning dawned, and the Rewa Scouts assembled on the river bank. Presently, the barges of the sugar company drew in to take them down the river and across the lagoon to the site of the rally.

In that moment, Isikeli found himself torn between two responsibilities. The inner conflict continued, and unnoticed, he slipped off the barge and took a short cut through the jungle.

[1] In 1932.

120

There was an important match that afternoon, and Isikeli felt he must stand by his team.

Somehow, when the match was over, the young player missed his launch that was to take him down to the rally.

Morning came, and Isikeli was one of the first on the jetty. The launch drew in. There were not many passengers, a number of Europeans, several Indians and one other Fijian. The sea was choppy. The boat rolled, and all on board were uncomfortably quiet.

Suddenly the silence was rent with a cry of alarm. The passengers came quickly together to see what had happened. Before they could even be told that a small European boy had become too venturesome and had gone overboard, a dark figure, fully clad, had gone in after him. Soon he was seen battling towards the little fellow. All on board had been shocked into inactivity. Terrified, they watched the little fellow—going down for the third time.

Next moment he found himself grasped by a strong hand. His first question was simply, 'What if there are sharks?'

Isikeli had hardly given himself time to take in that very real possibility. 'Oh,' he replied, 'there are no sharks here. 'The little fellow forgot his terror, and that was important. With Isikeli, it was *safety last*!

It took almost twenty minutes before the launch could be turned in that choppy sea, and brought alongside. Isikeli and the little fellow had been in the sea all that time. Exhausted, they were hauled on board.

One of the passengers approaching Isikeli, proffered a ten-shilling note. 'Take this.' 'Oh, no,' said Isikeli, 'I am a scout.'

The great church parade for the scouts was just commencing, as the launch, much delayed, arrived at Nukulau. As Isikeli hastened to join his friends, one of the launch passengers stepped forward and told of the gallant act he had just witnessed. The chosen speaker, Major Joske, straightway rose and told that great company before him how one of their own scouts had shown himself of strong courage that day.

Those who had cheered Isikeli's strength on the sports field, saw in him now strength of another kind, and they were honoured in him.

A year passed, and once more the scouts rallied at Nukulau. This time, in the midst of his fellow scouts, a coveted medal from Baden-Powell, the Chief Scout, was presented to Isikeli. *Again they spoke of gallantry, and that day the cheering of his brother scouts echoed and re-echoed like the cheering of the mighty football crowds many a time when Isikeli played a strong game!*

Thirty-one

God's Candlesticks

MATTHEWS, the young Englishman, was making his way north. It was a hard journey, and now he was almost at journey's end. He turned to his Maori friend accompanying him. 'Let us sit here,' he said, 'and rest a while before going down to them.'

Darkness was over the settlement of Kaitaia—not the darkness of nightfall. Titore, enlisting a powerful chief and his followers for war, had reached Kaitaia, for the purpose of inducing Panakareao, a renowned warrior, to join them. A war conference was at that moment in progress.

Aware of the presence of the two newcomers, two scouts were sent out to reconnoitre. They reported, on return, that one of the men was a Maori like themselves, the other a *pakeha* who could speak their language.

A small force was then dispatched to bring in the two strangers, and bring them in alive.

It was only when members of the force that surrounded them sprang from cover with the age-old Maori yells, that Matthews and his companion had any idea of their approach. The man in command of the small force had come supplied with cords to bind them, but as Matthews pointed out, they were going down to the *hui*[1] anyway. Courage was held in the highest regard by the Maori race, and the leader's face showed his respect. Leaving his captives unbound, he escorted them back to Kaitaia.

Along the flat at the foot of the hill, groups of armed natives came surging round, yelling and brandishing their weapons. As soon as one group retired, another filled its place. So menacing

[1] Maori Gathering.

was their aspect that the leader, mindful of his orders to bring in his men *alive*, ordered his guard to close in and beat off any who came too close.

As they reached the scene of the *hui*, pandemonium reigned; but in a short time this was brought under control by a word from Panakareao himself. He then turned his attention to Matthews and his friend, questioning them concerning their journey and its purpose. It was his purpose, he stated quietly, that they should be killed.

Matthews showed no fear, but said calmly: 'Not on the *Ra Tapu* (Sacred Day); besides, I have come a very long way to bring you a message. It would be a pity for you not to hear it.'

Yes, that was so, thought Panakareao; yes, they would hear his message first, and kill him afterwards. Certain of the company immediately got to work to heat the Maori ovens in readiness for the coming feast.

But Matthews's mention of the *tapu* of holy day had caught Panakareao's attention, for while his race had many *tapu* places and *tapu* things, a *tapu* day was quite new to him. He was curious to know more. This provided Matthews with a rare opportunity. Beginning with the sanctity of the sabbath, he went on to tell of Christ's mission, His crucifixion, and His glorious rising on the first day—that made this day so *tapu*, so sacred. It was all, of course, a new story to Panakareao, and he was greatly impressed. He was impressed also by the reverent telling of it by the man who stood before him.

Wonderful news! Was there any more to tell?

'Yes, much more,' answered the young Englishman.

Well, the feast would be postponed, and Chief Panakareao would hear more when he had finished his war conference.

The crowd clamoured for the word to kill the two strangers. Panakareao, however, put them off with, 'Not to-day, perhaps to-morrow.'

'But', they protested, 'the ovens are hot and all ready.'

'Then kill a pig,' ordered Panakareao, and turning to

Matthews, he said, 'We will hear more of your message another time; I am too busy now.'

The war conference was resumed; far into the night it continued. At long last the time came for Panakareao to give his decision. He refused to go with the visiting chief and his men. He had made up his mind instead, he said, to have the missionary Matthews and his friend return and settle in Kaitaia. And they would never come if he joined the war party.

Visiting chief Titore was bitterly disappointed at the decision. Missionaries, he retorted, were no good to a people. His anger, however, was appeased when Panakareao offered to allow any of his men to join up with his party if they so desired.

On the following day, which was Tuesday, Matthews found himself setting off to examine the site for the Mission Station. He was moved by the prospect, and delighted with what he saw of the surrounding country.

Days went by. At Panakareao's request he stayed on over the following Sunday, that the chief would be sure of observing the right *tapu* (holy) day. He was sent for again and again as opportunity offered, to relate more of the wonderful story.

In after years, Matthews sometimes spoke of the intense loneliness during that week of isolation from his fellow-Europeans.

There was great rejoicing at Waimate when he arrived back among his friends at the Mission Station, bringing with him the cordial invitation to move north and establish a station at Kaitaia.

✧   ✧   ✧

The years passed; innumerable obstacles still had to be overcome, the darkness in some parts was reluctant to yield. Panakareao had become a good friend of the Mission, and an active and earnest Christian. His wife, likewise, shared his new faith and service.

A time came, many years later, when it was suggested that one of the missionaries should be moved from among them. When Panakaraeo and his Maori people heard of it, they besought them with touching affection not to leave. To make doubly sure, the Christian chief, but so lately come out of the darkness, wrote to the Missions Committee in England. It was a beautiful letter. Translated, it read:

'Dear friends of the Committee, Our hearts have been made dark. We do not like to have our candlesticks taken away. If the Committee strive to take one of our candlesticks, we shall strive to keep him; and it will remain as a strife between us. . . . The old men were glad to have the young men come to occupy Kaitaia, and the young men came. . . .' The letter continued in this strain—all the way through, revealing their love for the 'candlesticks'—the young missionaries who had carried the Light to them.

A lovely nickname—'the candlesticks'!

❧   ❧   ❧

Recently a great bishop said to the World Alliance for International Friendship through the Churches at Geneva:

'In the black-out of the world to-day, God is seeking His children to bear His candles.'

Thirty-two

The Old Violin

AROUND some of our little churches back in the bush of Australia are beginning to cluster beautiful legends that hallowed memory and imagination have pieced together.

Come with me to a little stone church nestled in native pines near one of our great lakes. As you enter you will see before you, not an altar and cross, not even a communion table, but hanging on the back wall, an old violin and bow, and underneath it this inscription:

> The Violin of Joyful Joe, which
> in the Spirit of Christ, was dedi-
> cated to God, to the Keeping of
> His Love, and the Service of His
> Truth.

Our visit may be on a Sunday afternoon while divine worship is in progress. We do not fail to notice that the instrument has a strange influence on the worshippers, particularly on those who are getting old.

The anniversary service here is a strangely beautiful one. It is not the anniversary of the church—of which date nobody is quite sure—but of the violin! The difficulty of accommodating the congregation on that day is easily overcome by the women-folk and a few grandfathers sitting in the church, and men-folk clustering round the doorway and the open windows. By a free understanding, the sermon is always based on the same text about David and the house of Israel playing before the Lord on all manner of instruments.

But, you will ask, how do I know so much about it? The

answer is, I was the 'sky pilot' there nearly forty years ago. I was only what you would call a boy-preacher, and I was faced with a difficult problem. The church had no harmonium or instrument of any kind, and the congregation either could not, or would not sing. I did, not only the whole of the reading, preaching and praying, but also the whole of the singing. The folk, though quiet, were sympathetic. Indeed, no one has cheered me more than one old man among them. 'Joyful Joe', as he came to be called by those who loved him, called me 'Brother Hale', a form of address that pleased me very much, for I was then so young that I counted it an honour to be addressed as 'brother' by one so old.

One day when I was staying at his home down by the lake I saw something that I hadn't seen before. I should explain that I went often to his home, for his two daughters—they were over fifty and I was only a lad of eighteen—sort of mothered me.

This day, whilst my old friend was telling me how the Dear Lord—a term he used with great affection—had forgiven him and blessed him and guided him through the years, I noticed stacked up above on a high shelf, something that looked un-mistakably like a violin case, and I suddenly thought what a fine thing it would be if we had a violin down at the church. I said a little cautiously, 'A violin! You play it?' whereupon his customary cheerfulness vanished.

He said, shaking his head, 'That there fiddle? I've never touched it these forty years. Once I used it to play the devil's tunes in places of wickedness. I daren't touch it again. It would make me think of things the Dear Lord wants me to forget.'

I was sorry to have distressed the old man.

The following Sunday I had my first christening. Of course, I was nervous. But I remember the baby's name—it was Viola. I noticed that the mother of the little one pronounced it Veeola. I also noticed that the face of my old friend, Joyful Joe, was more radiant than ever. This, I thought, was only a natural expression of delight at the symbolical renewal of hope in the world. After the service, however, he buttonholed me, and said almost with a chuckle, 'And so you gave the baby a Christian name, and you called her Viola?'

'Yes,' I said, 'what of that?'

'Well,' he added, 'I'd like very much to see you to-morrow. Can you come?'

Of course I could. Next day there I was, I unsaddled my pony and put it in the loose box. Joyful Joe threw in a sheaf, and off we went to the house. On the kitchen table as we entered, what should I see but that violin-case—open—and in it the violin!

My old friend said, tapping me gently on the shoulder, 'Brother Hale, you gave a little baby a Christian name yesterday in the church, and called her Viola. Well, if you'll christen that old fiddle there, and call it a violin, I'll play it to the Dear Lord.'

Perhaps I should be ashamed to confess that I wondered what the Church authorities down in town would say, for a violin, though it may have a voice, isn't human. I quickly made up my mind, and said, 'Yes, and I'll do it now'.

So one of the daughters blushing with delight, placed a bowl of crystal water on the table. And moistening a finger, I touched the violin, saying, reverently: 'In the Spirit of Christ, I dedicate this violin (and I repeated it) this violin to God, to the keeping of His love and the service of His truth. Amen!'

It wasn't long before Joyful Joe and his old violin set the congregation singing—and it *was* singing. The attendance of the people gradually began to improve, so did the preaching, in that order of cause and effect.

One Sunday when we had a bigger congregation than usual, I was amused to have my old friend ask, 'Do you know how many we numbered to-day?'

'Yes,' I replied, 'forty, not counting the preacher.'

'You're wrong,' he said. 'There were forty-two counting the preacher—and the violin!' And we both smiled, and I apologized.

I

When Joyful Joe could no longer get as far as the church, he insisted on sending along his old violin. 'It has as much right to be there as anyone,' he would say, 'for it, too, is a member of the Church.' To honour this belief the congregation kept up the singing with the same earnestness.

When at last news came that the old man had gone, many gathered in the little church for a memorial service. It was a never-to-be-forgotten experience. Of course, we sang his favourite hymns, including 'In the Sweet Bye-and-bye', and it was during the refrain of that hymn that we had a strange experience. We felt—perhaps it was the workings of love and imagination—that we could hear Joyful Joe leading us with his violin. What I can say is, that if heaven is heaven, that dear old man with his converted fiddle is of that great company 'which no man can number'.

Thirty-three

'His Wonders to Perform'

THE old doctor had made up his mind on the unsuitability of the boy. 'I shall be glad to see the last of him,' he said, 'the boy's a menace and a pest!'

Certainly young George Brown had all but blown up the doctor's establishment with hydrogen gas, and had created no small stir in the streets with his phosphorus fire-bottles. It seemed clear by now that he had no special gifts for the medical profession. His engagement came to an end.

In a little time young Brown had fallen a victim to the dreaded Asiatic cholera raging through Barnard Castle. Somehow, he just managed to escape with his life—but one more escape added to his many. Mr. Brown always said that young George was destined for narrow escapes.

Soon he was leaving home for work in a large chemist's shop and bonded store; but it didn't last long. Hardly had his father taken his eyes off him, than he was off to Hartlepool to be apprenticed to a draper.

The drapery business in itself was not very exciting, but a spice of adventure came into his nights and days through an illicit trade in cigars and tobaccos and other dutiable goods brought over by captains of foreign ships. In exchange, they bought quantities of moleskins and printed goods to smuggle into their own countries. They found that they often needed just the sort of help young George Brown could give in stowing the goods. Everything had to be got aboard at night—an exciting and dangerous traffic. Young George's employer soon saw that it was much more to the youth's liking than standing behind a dull counter for hours at a time.

As for himself, George had now got a smell of the sea. In his secret heart he meant to make a bid for liberty the moment he could; the sea, everyone knew, spelt adventure. One difficulty lay in the fact that he was indentured, and must be prepared to risk being caught and brought back again.

When Christmas came round he made a bid for it, and got away in company with his unsuspecting employer, under the impression that he was going to visit his home folk. Arranging for his employer to call him early, they set out; he even managed to borrow ten shillings before they parted.

Never would young George Brown forget that adventure. He took a steerage ticket to London, and had only just left when they ran into one of the most terrible storms in living memory. Six worthy vessels went down in that storm. The tiny vessel on which he travelled kept passing wreckage. In imminent danger of foundering herself, she somehow managed to get into Lowestoft Roads when the weather abated. George felt so miserable that he was hardly able to reflect on his daring.

Soon he found himself in London without a penny. He hung about the wharves seeking work. He soon realized that his clothes were against him; it was apparent that he had never been to sea, and no one seemed over-anxious for the task of knocking him into shape.

He came on a captain who asked for his qualifications. Not over-impressed, he asked at last if he could cook. In desperation George answered, 'Yes!'

'All right, then,' said the captain, 'turn to!'

Below, on the clipper schooner engaged in bringing fruits from the Azores, George found that his first job was to cook a meal of roast beef, cabbage and potatoes. In his ignorance of just how to set about it, he put all three in together. To his boyish dismay, the cabbage cooked long before the beef. He stood it aside until the beef was done, and warmed it up again. This did not improve the meal. Happily for George, the captain and crew restricted their wrath to the greengrocer who had supplied the cabbage. With the next meal, George managed to reinstate the greengrocer in the captain's good graces. But tragedy lay just ahead. On Saturday night, orders were given for the Sunday dinner.

'Boy, you make us a good "plum duff",' ordered the captain.

'All right, sir', answered George but when he was left alone, he knew that his boyish inexperience had no hope of coping with such an order. That night in port, he made off. What the captain eventually got for his Sunday dinner nobody knows.

Soon George found a place on another boat; but before he could get away, a boy handed him a card with a warning: 'There's a longshore cove looking for you, and he says that if you don't go up to his house before to-morrow he'll have the police down after you.' How to escape from this fix? It seemed, from the name of a firm of London solicitors printed on the card, that his father's agents had somehow learned of his whereabouts. Escaping out of tight corners was one of young George's strong points.

In a very little time he was off to sea again—this time with his father's consent, on the understanding that he allowed him to find him a boat under the command of an old friend.

The world was unfolding very interestingly. He found him self on a large East Indiaman, under order to move soldiers to Gibraltar, and then the Cameronians to North Africa. But the wretched vessel had new sails, and none of her crew soon forgot the misery of being aloft on the topsail yards, trying to pit their puny strength against those new sails, frozen stiff. Somehow, the vessel got through.

Then occurred a misadventure that all but put an end to things for young George. With others he was working the cargo, and was sent up from the 'tween decks to fetch a light. Someone moved his ladder. He crashed. Save for the fact that his ladder fell across the combings of the 'tween hatch, he must have met his death. He suffered a broken leg in two places, with shock and bruises.

For many weeks he lay in hospital. When his ship was ready, she sailed without him; but later he came to think of it as but another narrow escape, for his captain and all hands were lost on the next voyage!

A little sobered, he made his way inland. He struck Montreal in time for the Gavazzi riots. From there he pushed on up the mighty St. Lawrence, through the canals and over the lakes. He found a promising job in a large general store. There he happened on a foolish youth. The two quarrelled. Young George found himself at some disadvantage, save when the battle was restricted to one of words. The big fellow, on one occasion, picked up a knife to strike. Tempers cooled, and nothing came of it.

A week or two later, however, the youths were out far from the town, pigeon shooting. They had only one gun between them, so they took turns. When it came George's turn, he loaded the weapon and took aim. Deciding, on second thoughts, that the pigeons were too far off, he dropped the firing-piece across his elbow, and as he did so, the hammer slipped somehow, and it exploded, the charge passing within a fraction of an inch of his young companion's head. Had he been shot, George must certainly have been proved guilty, because of the bad spirit existing between them. Both youths were sobered by the incident, and no more shooting was done that day.

Before many more narrow escapes had had a chance to befall him, young George was overwhelmed with home-sickness. Nothing would satisfy him but that he must work his way back, pick up a ship, and see the shores of England once more.

He shipped with an unusually rough crew. The ship's captain slept with his cabin door stoutly secured, and only moved about his vessel in the daytime, fully armed. An ordinary seaman, George owned the only sea-chest in the forecastle, the others had merely what was called 'a stocking full of clothes'. The vessel carried a heavy deck cargo which shifted dangerously in the strong westerly gales. Hours were spent at the pumps.

Then, as though their crossing had not been hazardous enough, their approach to the English shore was heralded by a nerve-racking experience. Things looked very ugly as all hands were called on deck, that morning just after dawn. The miserable ship was all but ashore on a little island in the Bristol Channel. So near had disaster come, that many of the rough seamen, with a sailor's superstition, refused ever again to sign on with a ship bound for Bristol. It *was* a narrow escape! But young George was home!

His people were very pleased to see him. But in no time, to their grief, he was straining to be off again. Nothing would do but that he must go to New Zealand—for no reason, seemingly, but that it was the place farthest from England. His father reasoned, but it was not easy to reason with 'wanderlust'. He insisted that this time George must go as a passenger, not as a seaman. George was ready to consent to anything, so long as he could get away.

With the passing of the long weeks and months, he came into contact with two great men, the Reverend J. C. Patteson, afterwards Bishop of Melanesia, and Bishop Selwyn, who held a class on the little vessel for any who wished to learn Maori.

How glad George was when they reached Auckland on its beautiful New Zealand harbour. The city, as yet, was very small, and sight-seeing did not take very long.

Taking with him a friend, he set off to trudge to Onehunga, a little place a few miles out. After they had gone some distance— young George smoking like a chimney—they met a man on horseback. As he got nearer they could see that he was a minister. Stopping him, George took out his pipe, and asked, 'Do you know a minister this way, called Buddle?'

'Yes,' said the minister on horseback, eyeing the questioner, 'I am Reverend Thomas Buddle.'

'Then you're my uncle,' said young George.

Never was a young wanderer received with more kindness and warmth than that young would-be sailor who came to the parsonage at Onehunga that day. All the good things of that simple home became equally his.

Before long young Brown realized that he must revise some of his standards; not that his uncle and his family ever preached at him, far from it. But he was a sharer in fine Christian living.

He got work, and began friendships with youths in the young men's Bible class at the chapel. Life began to take on a new colour.

Time passed, and incredible as it seemed to George when he reflected upon it, he was encouraged with others of his class, to offer himself as a young local preacher of the Methodist Church. This was followed by the suggestion that he should offer for the Christian ministry, or for special missionary work.

The very idea seemed, at first, out of the question. His friends insisted; nothing would do but that he must allow his name to come up before the quarterly meeting. A few were ready to risk a great deal on the evident miracle wrought in the young man's life; others were not at all persuaded of his suitability.

Eventually, young George Brown passed all the tests of the Church, and was marked down for foreign mission service.

One difficulty yet remained—he wasn't married! There wasn't much time, and the only young lady he had in mind,[1] lived at a Mission station to the north, some five or six days' journey away.

Undeterred, he set off, urging on his horse day after day, until the last evening brought him, travel-stained and tired, to the shores of a harbour nearest the Mission. The night passed miserably, his poor pony sharing his lack of shelter and food, and torture of mosquitoes. Still, the longest night passes. At dawn the rider raised his aching body from a hole he had scooped in the sand, and prepared to cross by canoe.

The Mission people were naturally surprised to see him, not less to learn of the important issue at stake.

[1] Sarah Wallis, daughter of Rev. James Wallis.

Sarah Wallis blessed his journey with her consent to become his wife. Just as he was leaving, a messenger arrived to say that the date of his departure for the Pacific mission field had been pushed on a few weeks. There was clearly now no time in which to return to Auckland. They had no certificate, and no wedding ring. But with the help of a magistrate living in the bush, and a young man who had already procured a wedding ring for his own wedding later in the year, even these difficulties were surmounted.

George Brown and his bride were young, and in the spirit to laugh at difficulties. In the company of a young brother of the bride and two Maori lads, they next set about the colossal task of getting themselves and their possessions by horseback to Auckland.

Most of the way they were obliged to camp out, at times with little more shelter than a native flax-bush. More than once they sought rest in a disused Maori hut, only to be driven forth by fleas. Their last night of the journey was spent on the coast in a furious gale which blew down their little tent and left them to the driving rain. It was not the kind of honeymoon most young ladies of those times thought of, but it proved a striking beginning for such a partnership of the years, filled with adventures.

Little did the worthy members of that early quarterly meeting realize that the day would come when they would be reminded of their decision, and the whole Conference of their Church rise to do honour to Dr. George Brown, outstanding pioneer missionary of the Pacific. No wonder laughter filled the courts of the Conference as that old decision was recalled: 'He is a good young man, but he is such a meek, mild, ladylike person that we are sure he has no spirit whatever that would make a missionary. He is utterly devoid, sir, of any self-assertion, and we therefore do not think that he is fit for the mission-work.' *So tremblingly had they sent young George Brown to his life work—forty-eight years in Samoa, the New Hebrides, New Britain, New Ireland, New Guinea, and the Solomon Islands!*

Robert Louis Stevenson confessed it one of his lifelong desires to write for the world the story of this great little man, his hero of the South Seas! *God moves in a mysterious way, His wonders to perform.*

Thirty-four

Pacific Raiders

THOSE in charge of the *Margaret Brander* had left Tahiti in an attempt to get native labour for the white man's plantations. The plan was to sail up to an island where they were not known. Soon the natives would come out in their frail canoes. Curiosity aroused, it would be an easy thing to induce them to barter; they could offer them muskets and rum, knives and odd bright beads and trinkets, and once they had lost their timidity, they could be invited down below to eat and drink. Whilst enjoying the food and drink, the hatches could be clapped on, and the vessel sail away at leisure. It would be easy enough and pay handsomely.

The villainous white men did not stop, of course, to consider the sadness that would descend upon the island people when the deserted canoes drifted back to shore, and the anger and resentment that would greet the story of the few remaining boys after the 'blackbirders' had left. Bereft, they would gather on the deserted beaches, straining their eyes until darkness fell.

❧   ❧   ❧

Days passed. The miserable prisoners found themselves crowded in the gloomy hold. Many of them, women and children, were too weak to offer resistance. Some could only fling their poor bodies against the hatches in a fever of fear.

After a while the hatches were opened and odd bits of food were thrown down to them. On board were a hundred and forty souls. The captain had lately added a new trick to his methods of getting a full ship—he had managed to persuade most to come on board on the pretext of going to work in Fiji. When he had suggested work in Tahiti, the island folk had refused to go so far, but once he had the poor wretches on board, he had not hesitated to laugh at his deceit.

Out a little, the *Margaret Brander* signalled the *Annie*, another vessel engaged in the evil trade. The captain begged the help of the sister ship. The *Annie* sailed in and out among the islands, until the full human cargo was complete, and the *Margaret Brander*, with three hundred and forty-five souls crowded into her hold, was ready to sail for Tahiti. Her captain had persuaded the supercargo of the *Annie* to change ships.

At first there seemed some risk that the human cargo might suffocate below. It seemed wise to let a few of them up at a time for air. 'Why should they die', the heartless captain of the *Margaret Brander* boasted, 'now that I've got them?'

'Better not let them up till we've cleared the islands,' suggested the newly arrived supercargo. The captain only ridiculed the idea.

When the morning came, the poor, miserable creatures from below spread out over the deck. Half-dazed in the sunlight, they caught sight of their home islands receding in the pale distance. At that, a mighty emotion seized them. There was no time to be lost. It was six o'clock in the morning. The supercargo was standing aft. One who had come up for a breath of air, suddenly seized an axe that was lying near, and coming up behind him, struck him dead. Panic broke. The captain, taken unawares, dashed below for his gun. Before he could take aim, it was wrenched from him, and he was struck down. The mate was the next to fall; two natives, forced members of the crew, also perished there in a matter of moments.

The island folk quickly scrambled aloft and cut the mainsail; they clumsily covered up the skylight, that the sailors should be hindered from directing their shots aright. One by one they took the wheel, in a desperate effort to run the ill-fated ship back to their island home. One by one they were felled. Finding it, at last, a seemingly hopeless task, they turned their energies instead to disposing of the remainder of the crew.

The bloody battle raged—for seven strenuous, terrible hours it raged—until those who remained alive were completely exhausted. Food and water were needed desperately. But the infuriated Dane, by now in charge, was unwilling to give up the struggle. 'No, no!' he shouted wildly, 'First we'll blow up the ship!'

His men reeled at the idea, but next moment found themselves laying gunpowder, especially heavily in those parts where the poor islanders were crowded together.

Sky and sea were blotted out in one terrific explosion! Above the confusion rose the voice of the Dane in charge: 'Up men, and at them with your cutlasses!' Numbers were blown into the sea, a few escaped.

Before night closed down on the grim scene, only two remained of that human cargo below. These were forced to help man the shattered vessel. The damage done to the hull was now seen to be less than at first appeared—much of the force of the explosion seemed to have been upwards and outwards.

The miserable survivors assembled on deck. Somehow they managed to get the vessel under weigh for Tahiti. With the confusion, and her mainsail gone, this was no easy task. Three months later an unrecognizable vessel limped into port.

Officials at Tahiti felt bound to make some sort of show, and they held a Gilbertian inquiry.

❦   ❦   ❦

The *Margaret Brander* refitted, soon set out unchecked on her traffic in human lives. What the sequel of the years would have been it is not hard to think. Mercifully, other powers began to bear down upon the 'blackbirders'. London Missionary Society missionaries were strengthening their influence in the Pacific. In time it became impossible for the 'blackbirders' to ply their evil traffic.

Thirty-five

'That Day!'

As the native schoolboys of Norfolk Island saw the clouded face of their young master, they knew that something really was amiss. The simple truth was that in their school was one boy who stubbornly persisted in bad behaviour.

Selwyn had spoken to him often, and he knew that he must speak to him yet again, and his heart was sad.

The hour came when, with all the strong tenderness of his heart, he attempted to check the unruly schoolboy. Facing Selwyn, the boy suddenly flew into a passion and struck his master a cruel blow in the face. All who saw it stood aghast. Selwyn said nothing, but walked quietly away. It meant that the youth must be expelled from the school.

Returning to his own island, the boy relapsed into the old debased habits of his people. Nothing was heard of him by the Mission folk for many years.

Then one day, long, long afterwards, a missionary at his work among these savage island people, was asked to visit a very sick man, and when he arrived he found the Bishop's old student. He was dying, and wished to be baptized. The name he had chosen for himself was John Selwyn.

'But why', asked the missionary, 'is it that you wish to have that name?'

'Because', the dying man replied, 'he taught me what Christ was like that day when I struck him.'

Thirty-six

The Brown Companion

THE runner from the District Officer panted out his message. Usaia quietly looked up from the work that he was doing. The fear that had gripped the islanders for many weeks had become a reality. 'Plenty Jap soldier 'e stop close to,' said the messenger. The Japanese were preparing to land on Usaia's island of Buka. Usaia was not afraid for himself, but war meant killing, and the teaching that he had given his people for twenty years had been 'You no killim man'. Didn't the Holy Book say, 'Thou shalt not kill'? Now there was a conflict in Usaia's mind— the teaching said one thing, the needs of the moment seemed to call for something else. It had not been easy to teach these erstwhile savages this hard thing. All the years he had kept on saying, 'You no kill 'im'. Now what was he to do? Of course there was his family, too—his wife and three daughters and two sons. He made his way hurriedly to the District Officer's house.

Racially, these to whom he ministered were not his people, nor was the island really his home. Usaia and his wife had come from Fiji to minister to these people, but with the passing of the years, they had *become* his people in a very real way. He had gone in and out amongst them. His voice, in more than one language, had become known among them, telling the good news. They had come to love him, to trust him; he solemnized their marriages, baptized their little ones, and buried their dead. His work was good, and his people happy and peaceful. The savagery of the old days had gone.

The District Officer's order was short and clear. Usaia was to be ready to go immediately with a European Government

officer and a little handful of helpers to warn the people to hide
in the bush.

Usaia was sad. Always the story of war was the same story—
stealing from the gardens, wrecking of schools and churches,
ravaging of villages, and if the invader chose, violence for their
womenfolk. There was no time to be lost.

Usaia hurried to tell his people what they must do; 'Go
bush,' he said, 'no go near Japs, no give *kai kai* (food).' Fear
stood in their eyes, and the exodus of the villages began. Men,
women and little children hastily gathered what little they could
carry, and made off for the hiding-places. Usaia did all he could
to work out plans for food and clothing, and getting all to
safety. But was there safety anywhere any more?

Plans were hastily made for the settlers. Usaia was promised
that his wife and family would be taken to safety, though nobody
at the moment had any idea what that would involve. In the
meantime they must share the fortunes of the people in the bush.

The European officer made it very clear that he meant to stay,
but Usaia, he said, was under no obligation to do the same.
Usaia, tall and lithe, a strong, full man, turned over his master's
words. Then he spoke his mind 'Usaia 'e belong you, *Kiap*.[1]
True me stop help 'im you.'

His decision made, he was given a rifle and instructed that he
must use it only in self-defence. Never for one moment had the
thought of doing anything else crossed Usaia's mind. Deeply
ingrained in his being was the higher law he gave to others:
'Thou shalt not kill.'

The Japanese started a man-hunt. They combed the steamy
jungle. For days at a time, Usaia and his master lay in hiding.
Sometimes the enemy were so near that they might have
touched hands through the jungle camouflage.

Days went by, and weeks went by. Now and again Usaia and
his little band of helpers moved outside the range of danger.
Then he would encourage the people as they crept out to meet

[1] Any Government officer in an administrative position.

with him, to join in worship. He even baptized their children
and performed their marriages under these strange conditions.
Sometimes as many as five hundred crept together for a Christian
service.

For long, Usaia had been a marked man. The invaders had
done their best to trick him. One day a Japanese officer who had
spent some time in Fiji, made his way to the head Mission
Station and left a polite little note on the school blackboard,
inviting 'Dear Usaia' to meet an old friend at a given spot.

Usaia was hunted relentlessly; he saw his wife and their family
subject to grave need. For days on end they were wet through.
Without food often, they shivered with cold in the mountains.
At other times they picked their way through the jungle.

Then Usaia and his master were trapped. A fight ensued, and
the white man was hit. Describing the action, Usaia said, later,
'Japs shoot, shoot all time. Me shoot plenty time. Me shoot to
make wounded. Me shoot here and here'—pointing to arms,
legs, and feet. 'Me no kill, you savvy. *Kiap* belong me hit.
Kiap say, 'Me done. You go." And me say, "No. Usaia
belong you. Me no can lose 'em you."'

Usaia's soft voice broke a moment, as he told of this action.
Then he went on, 'This fella masta 'e been die—Usaia 'e no
more look 'im 'em.'

But Usaia's own work, he knew, was not done; rather had the
load of a new responsibility been laid upon him. A third of the
little party had been killed, but there remained the exhausted
remnant, and hourly in danger. Following the master's death,
it was Usaia who fought off the attackers lone-handed. Those
who were with him knew that they owed their very lives to this
gallant rearguard action.

Unerringly, he led them through weeks of incredible hardship.
Often they were without food and drink. Always it was Usaia
who kept up their spirits and led them through the hazardous
adventures.

The wives and mothers of more than one lot of soldiers

K

fighting there in the jungle—Australians, New Zealanders, and Fijians—would one day see their menfolk because for Usaia it had always been *safety last*.

As he was later made to remember those days, Usaia would only smile his slow, sad smile. 'Japs no kill Usaia. By-and-by me die, long time after war, when me old Mission teacher.'

ᖍ   ᖍ   ᖍ

This is but little more than a torn page from the life of a very gallant Fijian, but it is a great page! Usaia's little family eventually managed to return to Fiji. Later he joined them there, but only to urge the authorities to send him back to his Solomon Island people in their need.

He has received the deep thanks of many who owe their lives to him. And now word has come that Usaia has been honoured with the British Empire Medal.

Thirty-seven

'In Dangers Oft'

THE teacher away up in the hills sat musing. His most precious possession lay open before him. It was an old worn-out Fijian Bible—a plain Bible with brown sheepskin cover. It had been sent out from England—a long, rough trip, lasting over six months. With others in the case it was dumped down on the wharf at Levuka. Later, the air was split with sounds of a hammer and the creak of the lid of a case being forced open. A great crowd of bushy-headed Fijians, young and old, had gathered. They were wildly excited as the missionary held up the new Book for them to see. A chorus of voices called out: 'Let me have it!'

But the missionary said, 'No, this one is for the teacher from the hills. He paid for it months ago, and has walked a long way to get it.'

So the Book was handed over to its master. He turned over the nice clean pages with delight. Then he wrapped it in a large handkerchief, placed it in the centre of a bundle of Fijian mats on a long white stick, and, putting this across his shoulder, began the long journey to the hills.

It was late at night when he reached his village. The news soon spread that the teacher had returned with the new Bible. The people crowded into the teacher's house and sat cross-legged, waiting for the teacher to finish his meal. Then he washed his hands in the earthenware basin which was brought to him by his little daughter. He unfastened the bundle of mats and the handkerchief in which the Book was wrapped. All the people, old and young, crept nearer to look at the new Bible which had been brought all the way from England, the white man's land.

'Now let us have prayers,' said the teacher, and someone commenced to sing the lovely old hymn, '*Jisu Ni lomani au* which, in English, is 'Jesu, Lover of my Soul'. Others joined in, and when the hymn was finished, the teacher turned over the leaves of his treasured Book until he found the stories of the lost sheep, the lost piece of silver, and the boy who left his father's house and went into the far country. The teacher then led his people in prayer, thanking God for His care, praying for the people in the hills who had not yet had the Gospel. Then all repeated together the Lord's Prayer.

As soon as the prayer was ended, Mere, the teacher's own little girl, about seven, took hold of the precious Book, and began to spell out some words.

Suddenly, through the stillness, there was a scream of terror. Everyone jumped up and shouted. 'It is war! It is war!' they called, 'the enemy has come!'

In a moment all rushed out of the house. They heard the blood-curdling war-cries of their enemies. Some of the village houses were already on fire, blazing fiercely in the strong evening breeze. The people scattered in all directions. Little Mere, still clutching the new Book tightly, was hurried away to her mother and together they made haste to hide in the long reeds some distance from the village.

The horror of that night will long be remembered, the wild cries and shrieks of terror, and the dull thuds of the heavy clubs as the fleeing people were struck down. The blaze of the burning buildings lit up the whole countryside. The roar of the fire and the bursting of the bamboo rafters in the fierce heat rent the air like gun-shots. Slowly the chant of the warriors died down as they dragged their victims away to the cannibal ovens in their own villages. Then there was silence—sad silence.

It seemed the night would never end, but at last the dawn came. Little Mere and her mother crept stealthily out of their place of hiding in the reeds. Alone, Mere's mother, the teacher's wife, went towards the smoking ruins of the village.

After a time Mere saw her returning, crying as though her heart would break. She had met some women who had told her the sad tidings that her husband had been killed and dragged away to the cannibal ovens. The whole village had been burned, and all the mats and baskets and wooden dishes had been taken or destroyed.

'Let us have prayers', said Mere's mother, and so saying, in her grief, she turned over the pages of the precious Book, and found in the wonderful fourteenth chapter of John's Gospel, the message which read: 'Let not your heart be troubled . . .'.

Little Mere and her mother, and the women who had returned with her, knelt down, and Mere's mother prayed God to forgive those who had ravaged their village and brought sorrow into their lives.

Some of the women baked yams in the smouldering ruins, and after the meal, the little party set off for a distant village nearer the coast.

They reached their destination about sunset. Mere's mother told the sad story. The only article of their possessions which they had saved, was the Fijian Bible to which little Mere had clung when they had had to flee from the village. Her mother now took it into her own hands reverently, and asked for a pen: 'This is her book, Mere Nasau. Is not this a brand plucked from the burning?'

Next day the little party journeyed on farther, to the Mission station. The missionary there had already heard of their plight. He did all that he could for Mere and her mother, and after some time, arranged for them to be taken to a distant island where their own people lived.

⚬   ⚬   ⚬

The tragedy behind her, Mere now went to school. In those days the Bible was the only reading book used in the village schools. Part of the work was to learn and repeat long passages. Mere, the little schoolgirl, of course, refused to be parted from her precious Book. When the missionary paid his annual visit to the island for the school examination, Mere won a prize for reciting the greatest number of chapters. It was a great occasion, and Mere treasured her Book even more.

Years passed. A young woman, Mere married a teacher named Josaia. They had not long been married, when there came a call for teachers to take the Gospel to New Britain. Josaia and Mere volunteered to go. Of course, they took their Book with them.

Not long after they reached their new home and work, Mere fell ill. She knew, as the weeks went by, that she could not recover. One day she called her husband, Josaia. She said, 'I am going. You are staying. Take my Book which we have read together each day; it has been light unto our path. Take it, read it, obey it.'

So Mere died; and was given a Christian burial in New Britain.

∽   ∽   ∽

After a time Josaia returned to Fiji. Often he took into the pulpit with him the Book which he and Mere had shared together.

At long last, he was appointed to a place up in the hills. One night as he sat alone in his house, an old man came to sit with him. He began telling Josaia stories of the early days, before the people of that district had become Christian. As the night wore on, story after story fell from the old man's lips.

'Yes,' said the old man, 'I remember when I was quite a young man. I went with some of my elders, and we attacked a village which used to stand over there. In the night we burned down all the houses, and we killed many of the people; one of them was the teacher.'

Silence fell between them. At last Josaia spoke. 'Do you see this Book?' he asked reverently, 'Well that belonged to that teacher you killed. His little girl saved it alone of all her possessions that night. Years afterwards she became my wife. We went to New Britain.' Josaia took up the old Book affectionately. 'She died there.' Silence fell between them. '*At last,*' he said, '*this old Book has come back to the place where it began its work in Fiji, and to the very people who killed Mere's father.*'

Thirty-eight

'The Everlasting Mercy'

THE old missionary grandmother sat in her chair. Her children and grandchildren constantly made the age old request: 'Tell us another story.' Much can happen in ninety years, and she had many stories to tell; but most often it was this story she told.

Two Fijian chiefs quarrelled bitterly, and the stronger raided his enemy's territory and took him prisoner.

He then made preparations to kill and eat Tuiciwi.[1] Before fulfilling his threat, he bethought himself of another chief with whom he wished to curry favour, so he sent a message to the chief, saying that he had Tuiciwi a prisoner, and the ovens heated and ready to cook him; he then added that he would like his friend to have the honour of clubbing the prisoner.

The second chief, on receiving the exciting news, immediately got ready his canoe. But before leaving, he recalled the rumour that the missionary, the Reverend Mr. Moore, had some American axes.

Without losing any time, he dispatched a boy to the missionary's house with the request that he would give him an American axe.

'What does your master want the axe for?' asked the missionary.

'Oh,' said the boy, 'Tuiciwi has been taken prisoner, and the neighbouring chief who holds him has invited my master to have the honour of killing him, and he thought he would like to have an axe rather than his club.'

Mr. Moore quickly prayed for guidance. Turning to the

[1] Tui-thiwi.

waiting boy, he said, 'Tell your master that this is the American axe I send him: listen carefully: "Blessed are the merciful, for they shall obtain mercy." The Gospel in which those words occur has just been translated.'

The missionary had the boy say the words over and over in his own language until he had them by heart. Then he sent him back to his master.

'Well,' asked his master, 'have you brought the axe?'

'This is the only axe the missionary sent', said the boy, and he repeated the words: 'Blessed are the merciful, for they shall obtain mercy.'

Frustrated, his master was furious, but he got into his waiting canoe, and taking the boy with him, set off for the island where the chief awaited his coming.

But his curiosity was aroused, and on the way round he kept the boy saying over and over the strange new words.

When he arrived he was received with much pomp: 'Come along,' said the proud chief, 'the ovens are heated, all is ready for the feast, and you are to kill Tuiciwi.'

Then the visiting chief told what had happened. 'This', he said simply, 'is the weapon I must use to-day', and he repeated in his astonished hearing: 'Blessed are the merciful, for they shall obtain mercy.'

With three dramatic words the old missionary grandmother loved to finish her story: 'So Tuiciwi lives!'

Though her listeners knew that story from start to finish, they never outgrew the thrill of it!

Thirty-nine

The Traitor Returns

A CROWD was gathered for a funeral on a little island of the Gilbert Group. No one could have guessed it, but it was a gathering to have far-reaching results. One of those present, Tanre,[1] had been openly jealous of the man who had just died; the next question upon everyone's lips was whether Tanre had not been responsible for his death.

Tanre was not only shamed in the presence of the funeral company, but before it had dispersed, he had fled in terror. Beru, of course, is not a big island, and it would have been impossible to remain hidden for long.

Now it happened, that as he slipped out in his canoe, a 'blackbirder's' ship came along. For poor, miserable Tanre there was no way of escape.

❧   ❧   ❧

With the longing for revenge strong within him, Tanre led the 'blackbirders' back to the very spot whence he had fled. They landed. The poor islanders were no match for the white man's firearms. They set fire to the houses, and when they had done all the mischief they could, they made off with their captives.

Raid followed on raid. Always Tanre was the chief helper; always there was the same tragic trail of looting and bloodshed.

But a time came when Tanre began to yearn to see his old island home. The 'blackbirders' had promised that when he had served them well, he would be taken back, but with the passing of the years they had shown no signs of redeeming their

[1] Tarn-ray.

promise. One day he clambered aboard, but unhappily, the boat put him down on a little island a thousand miles from his home. He saw the boat sail away.

Had he been stranded on the island a year or two earlier, his fate must have been a foregone conclusion. Now the people took the poor castaway into their homes and treated him kindly.

As Tanre shared the life of the people, he came to know something of the wonder that had changed their lives. In time, he too became Christian.

Then one morning a great ship loomed up on the horizon, and the cry went up '*Te Va'a Lotu!*' It was the mission ship, *John Williams*.

On board the *John Williams*, were some Samoan teachers whose great desire was to be set down on some island unvisited by a missionary. It seemed that Tanre's island was the very place they sought. Surely at last poor Tanre's prayer to get home was to be answered. The voyage, however, proved a test of patience; many stops had to be made on the way. As the ship ploughed on day after day, Tanre talked much with the Samoan teachers aboard.

In time, the *John Williams* came to a southern island of the Gilbert Group. The people saw the big ship approaching, and were filled with fear. They were sure it was the 'blackbirders' come again. And their fears were not allayed until a fellow Gilbert Islander, Tanre, set foot on shore to persuade them that the ship brought only friends.

A council was held, and at length the people declared themselves willing to receive a teacher. Encouraged, those aboard the *John Williams* sailed on.

At last Tanre's island hove into sight. The poor islanders were naturally terrified when they saw the big ship—the more so when one, scrambling aboard, saw Tanre there. *They* knew Tanre. The news passed from one to another.

The people quickly armed themselves; with their weapons edged with sharks' teeth, they presented a forbidding sight.

But friendliness and patience prevailed, though it was no easy task to persuade a people in such a mood that the great ship came in peace. In time the island people allowed the newcomers to go up to the meeting-place. They listened to their business. Very generously, Tanre's friends who remained—having heard his story with wonder—agreed to take him back.

As a sign of his new way of life, Tanre had earlier changed his name to Mattio. It was a great day for little Beru! *Tanre, the traitor, had become Mattio, the missionary—and in the good providence of God, the means of bringing Christianity to his own islands, the Gilberts!*

Forty

Love Travels Swiftly

THE tall, thin man with the lank, dark hair was troubled. In spite of all that he had done, war had now broken out among his Samoan friends. He was puzzled.

Disregarding his illness, he mounted his horse and went off among the folk of the villages to see how things stood. He found on all sides, activity and excitement which transformed old men into boys, and boys into steadfast warriors. Where would it end? The vivid imagination of Robert Louis Stevenson—'Tusitala', teller of tales—gave him no ease. Where would it end?

❧   ❧   ❧

The war itself actually proved short-lived and inglorious. But its ramifications were widespread. In the first engagement Mataafa's forces had tasted the bitterness of defeat.

The shadow of concern was on the thin, pale brow of 'Tusitala'. Was there nothing he could do, he wondered? Yes. He could do something for the humiliated prisoners.

So it was that as the prisoner chiefs came into Apia on the man-o'-war, they turned to one another in surprise: there to meet them the moment the man-o'-war docked, was this pale-faced friend of theirs. They knew the risks he ran. It was a fateful hour.

No sooner had he taken his leave of them, than his servants arrived labouring under great baskets of fruit and food. Said one of them: 'The heart of "Tusitala" is heavy. He has sent you these.'

'Tusitala' was very soon to learn other things that would

distress him. The prisoners were housed, it seemed, in a foul hole of a jail. As soon as 'Tusitala' heard this, he knew that he must do something about it. In a little time, he was having the place cleaned, and doctors in attendance to bind up the wounds that some of the men had borne from the battle.

And in the hearts of the poor, unfortunate prisoners was born a great gratitude. 'We must have a feast,' said one, 'and "Tusitala" and all his household must come.'

'Yes, a good plan,' said another, 'but of course, not enough.'

'We must load them with presents,' said a third.

But still—still for grateful hearts, not enough.

At last release came, and 'Tusitala' looked out of his window to see them wending their way up the steep path to his home.

They seated themselves, on entering, in Samoan fashion, upon the floor. The preliminaries of good form having been observed, out came their secret. 'Deep in our hearts', said one of their spokesmen, 'is the memory of what you have done for us. Now we ask of you one thing—that you allow us to build you a road. It shall be a good road, the best road we can make. It shall go from your house, and it shall go out to meet the road to Apia. And we will bear all the cost of it ourselves, and supply our own food as we work upon it.'

'Tusitala's' heart was deeply moved. Roadmaking among the Samoans, he knew well, was the most hated of all tasks. It was more difficult to get a road made in the island than almost anything else. And here were these men choosing to express their gratitude in this way! What could he do but allow them to go ahead.

So the great task was begun. And in a very short time *Ala Loto Alofa*—The Road of the Loving Heart, was an accomplished fact. Something lovely had been added to the annals of the South Sea Islands.

Forty-one

'Then Came the Dawn'

A COMPANY of small boys leaped and romped on the beach. Their shouts filled the air. To one among them, even in play, his fellows showed the greatest deference. He was the son of King Tanoa of Bau, who was at that moment making a visit to the island.

Even as they played, a message was brought to some of the little fellows that their fathers had been treacherously murdered. The news itself was grim, but immediately men rushed in upon the scene and seized the newly orphaned lads. A playmate of a moment before, now screaming with terror, was dragged to where the boy-chief sat. Club in hand, he was told to strike. His blows fell clumsily and ill-judged, but soon his little victim was dispatched. Putting down his club, the eight-year-old heaved a sigh. He had become a man; he had taken his first life.

Thakombau, the Fijian boy-chief, was from now on a figure to watch in the incredible drama of his island home.

Years passed quickly. The young chief became of very striking appearance, large, almost of gigantic size, his limbs were beautifully proportioned, his immense head covered with gauze, smoke-dried and tinged with brown. No garments confined his magnificent chest and neck. He looked every inch a chief.

Mr. Calvert, the missionary, found himself eyeing young Thakombau. What a trophy he would make for the Christian faith!

About this time a piratical tribe arrived, bringing spoil as tribute to the King, Thakombau's father. On such a high occasion, custom decreed that human flesh be obtained to furnish the ovens. Fourteen women who chanced to be out fishing

were this time the victims. The women were taken by surprise
and quickly overpowered in the shallow waters.

The grim news crossed to Viwa. 'Fourteen women are to be
brought to Bau to-morrow, to be killed and cooked for the
Butoni people.' Mrs. Calvert and Mrs. Lyth of the Mission
House were alone with their children at the time. Their husbands were away. What could be done? Every moment seemed
precious. Surely it would be more than life was worth to venture
into Bau. Yet, with all speed they decided on action. A canoe
was launched. Bau, they knew, would be in a ferment of excitement. Alas, they heard the first wild din of the cannibal orgy as
they made their way over the flats.

Landing, they rushed into the presence of the old King and
his son Thakombau. Both were obviously taken aback. But
the bloody butchery had well begun, nine of the victims had
already perished.

∾ ∾ ∾

As the death of the old King himself approached, a dark cloud
of apprehension hung over the people. The missionaries fervently clung to the hope that the ancient custom that decreed
that a man's wives must accompany him into the spirit world,
might be broken through.

The critical moment came. But his father's wishes were
already known to Thakombau. The missionaries had not so
much as arrived at Bau, before the death-drums were sounding.
Thakombau seemed embarrassed as the missionaries entered.
Their presence recalled the many talks they had had together.

King now, in his father's stead, there was no let-up in Thakombau's career of cruelty and bloodshed. The missionaries continually pressed their claims, but the only slender promise they
could exact from Thakombau was that he would consider their
claims for Christianity when he had at last subdued his enemies.
Blood continued to be spilled.

Time passed, and proud Thakombau came to know himself humbled in warfare. He was also smitten with a dread disease. It was a critical hour. What would Thakombau do? A message for him arrived from King George, the Christian King of Tonga, just then, warning him of plots against him, and urging upon his notice the claims of Christianity.

Day followed day, the people waited.

Then one morning the death-drums, that only ten days previously had sounded for a cannibal feast, sounded out for a great gathering of the people. Some three hundred made their way anxiously towards the strangers' house. This time the death-drums had called them to a Christian service. The day of the missionaries had come! Such a change of heart, as indicated by the King, seemed more than most could believe, but there was no doubting the reality of it.

King Thakombau now gave earnest heed to the word of the missionaries. He was careful in the keeping of the Christian sabbath; he procured a large bell with which to call the numerous members of his household to worship. Sacrificing wealth and prestige, he readily dismissed his many wives in favour of one. This was the new Christian way. So sincere was this erstwhile cannibal Fijian king, that at the end of three years of testing and instruction, he was presented, along with his wife, for Christian baptism. Was ever such a service held in the South Seas? One of those present wrote: 'In the afternoon the King was baptized. It must have cost him a struggle to stand before his court, his ambassadors and the flower of his people, to confess his former sins. In the past he had considered himself a god . . . now he humbled himself and adored his great Creator and merciful Protector. And what a congregation he had! Husbands whose wives he had dishonoured; widows whose husbands he had slain, sisters whose relatives had been strangled by his orders; and children and descendants of those he had murdered, who had vowed to avenge the wrongs inflicted on their fathers!'

Disputes still arose at times, but King Thakombau now

L

approached their settlement in a new spirit. By degrees, the old, evil ways were left behind in Fiji's bloody past.

As King, Thakombau's last significant act was to cede Fiji, his beautiful island home, to the great white Queen, Victoria. Along with a special message of love, he forwarded to Her Majesty his old and trusty war-club. With that gesture, club-law passed for ever from his blood-drenched land, and Fiji entered the British Empire.

The old Christian king died one morning in 1883, his last audible word a prayer 'Hold me, Jesus! Hold me, Jesus; my faith in Thee is firm!

And so came the dawn to Fiji!

Forty-two

Jungle Trek!

THE wife of Moses Kopiiku, the teacher, was busy in her leaf house. Her husband was away; he had gone, as his custom, to the monthly class-meeting thirty miles off. She hoped he would be back again early in the morning; the truth was she needed his help. While he had been gone a woman in the village had died, and after her death her little newly born babe had been roughly handled by some of the village people. They had wanted to be rid of him. Already he bore blue marks on his tiny body where they had tried to kill him.

'Stop! Stop!' cried the teacher's wife, 'You cannot do that!' She was only just in time. An old woman was already knocking the little newborn one on the back of the head with a stone.

'Stop!' she cried, 'I will take him.'

But the people were furious. Always this had been the fate of little orphaned babes. What business had she to interfere?

She did interfere; she knew a better way. Caring nothing for the anger of those about her, and the personal risk that she ran, she grabbed up the little one and ran into her house. She had children of her own.

Once inside her cool leaf house, the tiny morsel of humanity stopped his crying. She could not keep him always, but she had saved his life. How she wished her husband would come. He must go back and take the news to the missionary's wife. She was the mother of all little helpless babes in these parts.

At last Moses came. He looked tired. But as soon as he heard the pitiful story, and looked on the little one, the sixty miles he had covered in two days seemed as nothing. Yes, he would return at once.

The missionary and his wife were surprised beyond measure to see Moses back.

'I want you to give me a bottle and a teat and a tin of condensed milk,' he said.

'Whatever do you want those for?' asked the missionary's wife. Soon he was telling her the story of the babe.

No, he could not stay; he must go back at once.

On his arrival, his wife quickly attended to the little motherless one. Then once again, Moses turned his face to the track. Up hill and down it wound, across logs and streams to the missionary's house. So he made his fifth trip, this time going more gently, because of the tender nature of his burden, stopping now and again to rest and feed his little charge. It was a curious sight to see the dark son of a savage armed, not with shield and battle-axe, but with a feeding-bottle and a tin of condensed milk. At last he came in sight of the missionary's house. Not much longer now. He peeped at his little charge. No, not much longer now.

Soon the little one was given over to the keeping of the missionary's wife—added to her already large family of orphans.

And Moses? He had then to turn and make the trip once again over those taxing thirty miles to his own home—six times in a week—*and four times thirty miles to save the life of a little helpless babe!*

As the missionary's wife bent over the little one she was heard to say, 'Truly, the Friend of little children has worked His miracle of love and tenderness here!' She added, 'Life becomes precious only where His touch is felt'.

Forty-three

The 'Brothers'

THE old chief had seen many things to cause him fear, in his jungle life, but nothing of this kind before.

The two Solomon Island lads before him were 'brothers', and visitors to his village. He could not know, of course, that theirs was a great brotherhood of Christian lads, working two by two through the heathen villages, preparing the way for others who would come.

The old chief could not know these things. He was uncertain about these newcomers; he thought it best to lock them up for the night. Were they enemies or friends? By morning he had decided, and he had them brought forth to be killed by order of the 'spirits'. The lads stood before the old chief.

Suddenly he stepped back. 'Two brothers came in last night,' cried the chief, 'two brothers were brought out this morning; but now I see *three* brothers. These have another who travels with them!'

The two young lives were spared, and a new field of service opened.

'*These have Another who travels with them.*' The lads wondered at what had happened. How was their secret uncovered to the heart of the old chief? They did not know. Only one thing they did know—that their Lord and Master had never once in their dangerous life broken His promise to them: 'Lo, I am with you alway, even unto the end.'

Forty-four

Dawn Attack!

Soon it would be morning on a coral island. On the reef the long rolling waves, breaking gently, gave no hint of what was to happen. The palms, catching the light, lent grace to the scene; the hibiscus, the bright oleander, the frangipani, colour and fragrance. Nature was hardly awake as yet, the dawn had hardly come. The hill-topped island of Atiu seemed too fair a spot from which to make such an attack.

Then, of a sudden, fierce shouts rang through the air. Sounds of blows mingled with groans of pain. As undertone to the martial chanting of the warrior's song were the wailing of the women, and the frightened cries of the children.

It was a great occasion on Atiu island. Rongo-ma-tane was leading out his warriors to fight against the inhabitants of the smaller islands. Sacrifices had been made; human victims slain and offered, accompanied by weird dances and strange cries to Oro, the god of war, and to Tane, giver of food and protector of the land.

The great war-canoes lay waiting. Chief Rongo-ma-tane and his mighty men had already arrayed themselves in their fighting masks. At a word, armed fearsomely with spears and clubs, the warriors would rush down to the beach. The giant canoes but awaited the word. Before they could be launched they must, of course, be served with rollers. Miserable creatures taken on a previous raid, and bound hand and foot, must be cast down on to the beach under the bows. At a shout the heavy craft would be pushed down over the human rollers into the sea.

Now the cry came from the warriors in the canoes as they faded away into the distance: '*Kia Mate! Kia Mate!*' (Kill!

Kill!) Presently they would be out of sight—gone on their dread errand.

Too well those who waited behind knew what savage warfare meant. If Rongo-ma-tane should prove victorious, his return would be accompanied by an orgy. If, as might be, he and his proud warriors came not back, others as fearsome would come ere many nights, thirsting with revenge.

The old men, the women and the children alone remained now. The old men could go no more; so they lifted up their cracked voices to boast of past exploits, and to bespeak the assistance of the gods.

The sun was mounting up. The warriors had well gone.

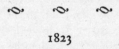

1823

Three years later, another dawn was breaking on Atiu island! Two of the island's fishermen, coming back early, had brought strange news. The previous night, far away out at the going down of the sun, they had spotted a strange ship on the horizon. It was a startling piece of news; they hastened back to share it. They must not be caught sleeping. Spears and clubs were speedily got out, and men sent off to the cove for the great canoes. Who knew whether these were enemies or gods?

In the midst of the bustle and flurry, of a sudden, up spoke an old grey-haired man. He was of those who knew the ancient tribal stories. Saluting his chief, he began impressively 'Rongo-ma-tane, high chief, hear me! The story that these fishermen have told is not strange to me. When I was young, there came just such a canoe with masts that reached into the skies. The men who brought it had white faces, and their chief was one by name of Kuki.[1]

'We thought them gods; at first our bravest were afraid. But by and by, one of our men paddled out to the great canoe, and

[1] Captain Cook.

heard there brown-faced men speak as we speak. Through them, our people learned that Kuki and his men wanted coconuts and water. Our people gave to them. Kuki's men gave in return, knives and axes and strange, flat things, called mirrors, in which one could see his face as in the still pools among the rocks. Then were all happy. My father was one of those who exchanged his coconuts for the new things. Many times he told me of it. "Some day", he said, "the great white chief and his big canoe might come again." It might be', he murmured, breaking off his story, 'that this is Kuki come again. Let us take our weapons, but let us not be over-ready to use them. These are my words. Let us show ourselves friendly to these great ones who come.'

As he seated himself once more, a low murmur of approval greeted his words. When the mind of the assembled people was clear, Rongo-ma-tane arose. 'It is well,' he said, 'I myself will go to meet the great white chief when he comes!'

Just then—as the dawn was broadening—a runner from the beach burst in upon them with the news that the great canoe from beyond was even now in sight. Immediately Rongo-ma-tane, suitably arrayed, stepped out into his canoe. He was paddled out.

When at last he did clamber on board, he found not Kuki, as he had expected, but the missionary John Williams and his teachers. More amazing still, on board the great canoe was his fellow-chief, Tamatoa, from the not distant island of Aitutaki. And he could hardly believe his own ears when Tamatoa told him that he and his people had forsaken the gods of the ancestors.

Last doubts only vanished when his fellow-chief piloted him down into the hold. There were the most feared of the gods, lying like so many pieces of worthless wood.

'What!' exclaimed the incredulous chief, 'you have done this? You have slighted Oro, and he has not destroyed you? You have burned Rongo, and he has not sent you a tempest? And you have thrown down Tane, and he has not sent you a blight on all growing things?'

'Yes,' responded the glowing Tamatoa, 'we have done all these things, and no evil, only good has attended us. They are all laid low—the gods of our ancestors. Long we feared them, but we were deceived. Stay, and we will tell you yet more wonderful things.'

And Rongo-ma-tane, in something of a maze, stayed. All that night he slept but little. Too many strange new things were going round in his mind.

Next day was Sunday, and John Williams, gathering his teachers, preached a powerful sermon from the book of Isaiah, especially for Rongo-ma-tane. He listened, and would never forget the surprising words:

'Then shall a tree be for a man to burn, and he takes it and warms himself; yea, he kindles it into a fire and bakes bread. Yes, he makes a god, and worships it; he makes it a carved image and falls down to it.'

> *He burns a part of it in the fire;*
> *With a part he eats flesh.*
> *He roasts meat and is satisfied:*
> *Yea, he warms himself, and says,*
> *Aha, I am warm, I have seen the fire:*
> *And the rest of it he makes into a god!*

Rongo-ma-tane, great chief, ejaculated, '*E tika! E tika!*' (It is true, it is true!)

Two days he stayed, and when the third morning dawned his mind was made up. Though his gods had eyes, they could not see, ears, they could not hear, hands had they but they were powerless to help.

When John Williams came up on deck, Rongo-ma-tane rushed up with, 'Give me axes! Give me axes!

'What do you want axes for?' asked John Williams.

'To go ashore and destroy the *maraes*,' he answered, 'to hew down the best trees in the forest, and to build a church for the worship of the one true God.'

So a great victory was won that dawn!

John Williams later discovered that Rongo-ma-tane was chief also of some adjoining islands. These were the unfortunate people against whom the dawn attack had been made a few years earlier. Now the proud one was leading the missionaries over his old tracks, on a mission of mercy and peace. Verily, the dawn had come!

∾   ∾   ∾

1912

Once more it was dawn. Shouts of happy play rang through the air. A crowd was gathered on Atiu. The missionary who had come in the steps of Williams, was visiting his people. One of the early events of the day was a game of cricket.

The day wore on. After sundown it was rounded off with a great meeting. Never would they forget it. Long before the bell had finished its ringing, the people had gathered. The missionary had brought with him native teachers who had served as missionaries in other islands, and after a brief rest, were returning. They told of villages they knew that had not yet been reached by the Gospel; of savage people amongst whom war and fear still reigned. The company listened spell-bound. Then the last teacher rose to speak. He told of many who had joined them from Rarotonga, from Aitutaki and other places. Then dramatically he turned to face the young men in the front rows. 'How many have gone out from Atiu?' he asked. Silence reigned. Some in that great company felt shame that not one had gone from Atiu.

Again the young teacher—remembering their cricket match of the morning—uttered his challenge: 'Who will break the duck's egg for Atiu?'

All waited. There was a movement. Tumupu,[1] the young son

[1] Too-moo-poo.

of the present Rongo-ma-tane, rose to his feet. With gleaming eyes, he faced them. 'I,' he said, 'I will break the duck's egg for Atiu!'

All eyes were fixed on him. 'And who,' he challenged, 'who will come with me?'

A young man in another part of the company stood up. 'I will go,' he said quietly, 'I will go!' Presently a second volunteer stood.

Verily, a new dawn had come—a dawn of responsibility!

∾   ∾   ∾

1917

Again the people of Atiu Island were assembled at the call of the bell.

Tumupu, son of Rongo-ma-tane, had returned. The five years of preparation for his new task were at an end. It was a sacred moment. Tumupu rose to speak. He reminded his people of that gathering five years earlier, when he and his two young friends had stood to pledge themselves to a new service.

The morning came, and the people gathered round the young man and his friends as they took their leave at the landing-stage. Many would never forget that hour. The cry in the old days had been, '*Kia mate! Kia mate!* (Kill! Kill!)' Now the cry wafting across the waters, as their young friends took their leave of them, was, '*Kia ora na! Kia ora na!* (May you live!)'

So Tumupu—in the line of old war-like Rongo-ma-tane—set about the waging of a warfare against evil and darkness. It was God's dawn!

Forty-five

'One Increasing Purpose'

THE young Solomon Islander had finished his two years at a college in New Zealand. He had made many friends; they loved his black skin, glistening teeth, and smiling face. As he stood to speak a last word to those gathered about him, he was tempted to use a phrase he had lately picked up: 'One Increasing Purpose.' But there was no need to use it—it was implied in all that he said. There was no need to use any picked phrases for the rapt attention of that group. Simply he told his story. Once, long ago, a band of Solomon Island warriors left Roviana (Munda) on a head-hunting expedition to the island of Ysabel. They raided a chosen village, killed everyone, and beheaded their victims. The heads of enemies had great soul value, and it was believed that the more heads one secured, the better time he would have when he passed into the spirit world.

The raiders set about counting up the heads. There were three hundred. Presently, they heard the faint cry of a little baby. in a nearby hut they found him lying amongst the de-capitated bodies of his parents, brothers, and sisters. One little baby! Just what they required for the time-honoured custom of sacrificing an infant after a successful head-hunting raid!

A great crowd awaited their return to share the glory of their success. The warriors lined up on the beach; word was given, and the tiny babe was thrown into the air. Each warrior gave him a squeeze, and tossed him up for the next in the row to catch. So unusual was it to hear the cry of a baby in the Solomons—a baby seldom cries for fear of attracting the enemy—that if one should cry whilst being tossed from warrior to warrior, it was accounted a message from the spirit-world.

It happened that, as the warriors celebrated their victory, there waited in the crowd an old woman who, as a baby, had been saved from death. She watched the proceedings closely. From one to another the tiny babe was tossed. Then suddenly, almost to the end of the row, he cried. She immediately came forward and took charge of him.

Weeks passed, and the little one's bruises were well again. He grew, and in time became a slave of the high chief of the district. By the time he had reached manhood, he had earned great fame as a head-hunter. So highly did the high chief think of the prowess of his slave that he purchased a young wife for him. By and by he had a son of his own, but the young mother died at the child's birth. It happened that just as the little one was being thrown into the grave with his mother, as was the custom, that they might go together into the spirit-world, a woman from nearby jumped in and took him into her arms, saying, 'I will look after him!'

The boy grew up, and became a famous head-hunter, and in time also the father of a small boy.

As the little fellow followed his father about, he too, in his own childish way, dreamed of the day when he would become a famous head hunter. But that day never came. In the interval, Methodist missionaries had come to Roviana, and his father, who had become Christian, sent him to school. He would have rather played about with the other boys, a naked, dirty little savage. Often he ran away from school, but as time went on, he became more friendly with the strange white people. When not climbing the mast of the Mission boat, and diving feet-first into the sea—a thing he loved to do—he would stand at the little cabin door of the boat, watching the interesting things that went on inside there.

As he stood there one day, quietly watching, someone asked him if he would like to become a teacher some day. 'Yes', he replied, he would like to become a teacher; asked if he would like to become a missionary, he replied in the same way. As suddenly realizing that perhaps he had sounded over-ambitious, he had added: 'One thing I know, I'm going to be a Christian.'

∽   ∽   ∽

The young speaker paused a moment, and looking round that college group, quietly added: 'Thank God, I am a Christian to-day. I am he whose father was saved, as a babe, from being buried alive, and whose grandfather was saved from the warriors on the beach!'

Belshazzar Gina, affectionately known as Gina, returned to serve his Solomon Island people, and eventually became the first native minister of the Methodist Church.

But since those happy days, war has come. It has not always been easy to follow the fortunes of Gina during the intervening years, but four vivid pictures have been pieced together.

I

After the American forces had landed on Guadalcanal in August 1942, the Japanese set up a base at Gizo. Behind the bare headlines about the bombing that drove them out, there is a thrilling story.

On three dark nights of one week, a number of natives visited that area in a canoe. One of them quietly and courageously swam under water close inshore. He carried a piece of coconut frond in his mouth, so that if the enemy watchers should see any movement out on the dark water, they might think it was a floating coconut or even a crocodile. Thus they gleaned the information they sought about the enemy's troops, dumps, and gun-positions. They carried their information to a radio unit a hundred miles away. In due time, Allied planes came over, and the base was destroyed.

II

Months later, two natives were posted to watch from a high look-out. The Japanese were building an air-field on Munday.

Days went by—not for one moment was their watch relaxed. Turns were taken in watching and resting. The approach to their look-out was a steep path up the coral cliff. It was a splendid look-out, but one day, to their horror, one of the boys looked over the edge of the cliff to discover an enemy patrol near the top. Hastily he roused his mate, and they made a dash out of the house only a matter of seconds before the Japanese came in. Finding evidences that the house had been lately occupied, the Japanese there and then set about wrecking everything within.

But the two island boys were not at all satisfied that they had finished their job. Presently, they returned, and went on with their watching.

III

The Japanese invaders were establishing their base on Viru Harbour. Four native lads determined to gain a knowledge of the number of enemy barges and the whereabouts of the radio station. It would not be easy. That, the leader of the little party knew. It was dangerous, but they were to await his return, he said; he would make his way down into the camp alone. But the others would not hear of his going alone. All would go, they said. So, disguising themselves—two went naked except for the 'T-piece', two wrapped sacking round their loins, and rubbed lime into their hair, covered their bodies with dirt, and chewed betel-nut to make their teeth red and their mouths filthy—they went off down, ostensibly to gather foodstuffs and to look at their houses. They agreed that however they were cross-questioned, they would know no English, not even Melanesian pidgin.

The Japanese spied them. The commander had his officers closely question and cross-question. Nothing could they get from the lads. One of them, showing more interest in things than the officer thought good, was cuffed across the face and knocked down. After some hours the commander was ready to let them go. 'Only wild Kanakas,' he classed them, and wrote a pass and gave it to his guards, with instructions to take the wild natives to the outpost, and let them go.

On the way, the lads somehow persuaded the guards to let them gather taro roots from a nearby garden. They contrived to take so long over the simple task of gathering and scraping taro, that the guards grew weary, and ordering them to take the pass to the sentries when they were ready, went back to camp. Once they were out of sight, the taro-collecting came to a sudden end, and the boys escaped into the bush.

The information thus gleaned, enabled the Americans to destroy the barges and radio station.

IV

A missionary who had served in the Solomons was able to return for a brief time as Chaplain to the Forces. Everywhere the natives gave him a great welcome. The people of one place in the Roviana Lagoon hastily gathered when they heard that he was at hand. Seizing the opportunity, they gave him a bag of money, with instructions that he should somehow get it to New Zealand. It was their annual thanksgiving offering, and amounted, they said, to sixty-eight pounds ten shillings. The padre was not able to count it just then. Several days later, when back at his base on Vella Lavella, he found time to check it, and found it as the people had said, sixty-eight pounds ten shillings. One thing he found within, which gave him great pleasure—an envelope containing notes and coins, with this message: 'Donation from B. Gina and family, sixty-six dollars and four shillings—twenty pounds!'

෴   ෴   ෴

The young native who swam under water during those dark nights at Gizo, who watched with his companion at the Munda look-out, who was slapped over the face by a Japanese officer when he led the little party down into the Viru Harbour camp, who wrote the message on his thanksgiving envelope, were one and the same—Belshazzar Gina, whose father and grandfather were saved in babyhood!

In such one cannot but feel the pulse of 'One Increasing Purpose'!

Forty-six

'Love Ever Gives!'

Love ever gives—
Forgives—outlives—
And ever stands
With open hands. . . .

'WE should reach our destination in a couple of days, if things go well,' said Goldie to his friend Rooney. 'If not, we may be a couple of weeks drifting about in this tropical heat, waiting for the wind.' The little *Bondi* was a sailing-vessel of a paltry three tons draught, with a cabin in which it was quite impossible to sleep.

The thoughts of the two young pioneer missionaries were constantly of the people of Kuboro. Of late, these people up in their fortified mountain village had shown some readiness to receive a teacher; so it seemed wise to pay a visit and see how things stood. Hitherto, they had been decidedly hostile; even now they might change their minds.

On landing, the two young missionaries prepared to have *Lotu*.[1] When the moment came, there were only men present, and all armed! The young white men kept their eyes on all who had gathered. It had been Rooney's idea to have *Lotu*; when he had called on his astute young friend to pray, he had replied, 'Oh, no, Ray, you pray—I'll watch'. Admittedly the appearance of the congregation did not inspire confidence. But the visit passed off without any untoward happening.

∾   ∾   ∾

[1] Christian worship.

In due course it was thought desirable to call again at Kuboro. Through an interpreter, Mr. Goldie this time, pleaded with the people to show their former readiness to accept a teacher. The several hundred people of the stoutly fortified hill village made no response. Goldie was disappointed with his efforts. There seemed nothing for it but to put out to sea once again.

On the tiny vessel, however, was a Christian Samoan youth named Muna. As they talked over the position with the hill people, Muna pleaded that he might be left behind to see what he could do.

At first his friend Goldie refused to listen. 'They will only kill you, Muna,' he replied, 'and what use would that be?'

Silence fell between them. Muna said that he felt it was God's will that he should stay. As he showed no sign of yielding, Mr. Goldie at last gave in, and sent him ashore with a dinghy, a tin of cabin biscuits, a bag of rice, and a cooking-pot.

As the little *Bondi* sailed away, the brave Samoan was seen standing on the beach, and they heard him call that he was now like the birds, and the animals in the bush, with only the sky to cover him.

That was the last that Muna's Mission friends saw of him for some time.

    ❧   ❧   ❧

One evening, much later, Mrs. Goldie (Marama) returning from a medical trip to a far village, saw approaching her along the beach in the half-light, an emaciated figure. She was at a loss to make out who it might be. The next moment, the poor creature before her was taking up her hand and kissing it. It was Muna.

'What have they done to you, Muna?' she asked, with tears.

Gradually, and without bitterness, his story came out. He had tried, day after day, to hold *Lotu* amongst the people, he said, but the more he tried to help, the angrier they became. At last, some men of the village took two logs and bound them together. Then they cast Muna adrift on the rough, improvised raft.

As he left the shore in this helpless state, several alligators came dangerously near, and he saw sharks. As if divinely protected, nothing actually molested him. He drifted on, exposed to the cruel tropical sun by day, and to the great rains.

At the end of days—just how many, Muna could never clearly remember—some natives returning from a turtle-hunting expedition, spotted an unusual object floating in the distance. Out of curiosity, they paddled towards it. The unusual object was Muna on the raft.

Excited, they tried to talk to Muna, but they could make nothing of his jabber. All that he could say sounded like 'Kolini' and 'Loviana'—his version of Goldie and Roviana. The word 'Loviana' must have penetrated into the consciousness of the strange men, for after a little time, they cut the ropes which bound him to the logs, and lifted him into the bottom of the boat. Exhausted, he lay there.

Then they turned their canoe, and paddled the fifty-odd miles, out of their way, to Roviana. And so Mrs. Goldie had come upon him.

Muna's Mission friends carried him up the hill, and made him comfortable.

With the passing of time, Muna's poor, emaciated body regained its strength. But no sooner did he feel his strength returning than he grew restless, begging an answer to his one question: 'How long will it be before I can go back and try again?' *Safety?* That was Muna' *last* consideration.

❧   ❧   ❧

Mr. Goldie, after a time, managed to acquire an island a little way out from the steep mountain village where the people had treated Muna so badly.

There brave Muna returned to serve!

Love ever gives—
Forgives—outlives—
And ever stands
With open hands.
And while it lives,
It gives.
For this is Love's prerogative—
To give—and give—and give.

Forty-seven

'The Brown Disciple'

THE church was hushed and still; it was the service of Holy Communion. Those reverent Maori people who knelt to take the sacred elements of bread and wine, symbol of the broken Body and the shed Blood of our Lord, were aware of a slight stirring among their number. One was seen to withdraw from the semicircle before the communion-table and go to his seat at the back of the church.

In a little time he had returned to his former place, and now knelt to take the Sacrament.

Later, in answer to a question, he explained his curious conduct to his fellow-disciples, and long would they remember his words: 'When I approached the table I did not know with whom I should have to kneel,' he began reverently. 'Then suddenly I saw that I was next to a man who years ago, slew my father and drank his blood. That man I had sworn to kill the moment I met him. So I went back to my seat.

'But as I sat there, I saw in the spirit, the sanctuary on high, and I seemed to hear a voice saying: "Thereby shall all men know that ye are My disciples, if ye love one another." That made a deep impression on me. And I thought I saw another sight, a cross and a Man nailed upon it; and I heard Him say, "Father, forgive them, for they know not what they do".

'*Then I went back to the altar.*'

Forty-eight

'And all the Trumpets Sounded . . .'

THE sun shimmered on the sea, and beat unmercifully on the young white man. He had only been on Vella Lavella a few days. His hastily constructed hut was the simplest thing imaginable.

A few paces from it this morning, he noticed hiding in the darkest corner of a native hut, a little fellow about twelve years of age. He was suffering from a painful inflammation of the eyes. Again and again he had tried to get a glimpse of the strange white man. It was no use; the light was too strong.

The young man, Nicholson, returned to his rough hut, and prepared a bowl of warm boracic lotion. For an hour he bathed those raw eyelids. Then he made a second trip to 'headquarters', broke open a case, and returned with an old celluloid eye-shade.

Next morning he went to the little fellow again. He led him to his hut this time, and bathed his poor eyelids. And day after day, morning and evening for over a fortnight, he repeated the process. There was something indefinable about the little chap; at first he had been shy, but gradually he became more trustful of the strange white man. And then there was begun a friendship which grew into a loyal devotion and ceased only with death.

The parents of little Bula were outstanding personalities—his father, a notorious head-hunter, and because of his temper, greatly feared among his people; he also possessed knowledge of the use of native herbs. His mother had hypnotic powers, and practised witchcraft.

The days of little Bula's childhood, of course, were very different from those of a child in a Christian country. Baby life had to struggle against its sicknesses in filthy surroundings, and subject to the whims of heathen parents. On one occasion, Bula's father, in a fit of temper, tied him up in a tree, and leaving him, callously went off on a fishing expedition of several days. Happily, his mother found him in time to save his life. Inter-tribal fighting among his elders was common; much time was taken up with their head-hunting expeditions. Houses were hurriedly built and frequently changed. A house had only one room, in which all the family, visitors, and all the pet pigs and dogs of the family slept. In such surroundings little children were left a good deal to fend for themselves, and matured early.

Little Bula became cook-boy to his new friend, 'Nikolo'. He scarcely knew how to 'cook' water, it is true, but he was a wonder at making a fire. When 'Nikolo' came out to cook the meal there would be a fire raging fit to cook an ox. Meal-times were full of queer mistakes in early days. The tiny hut had only one shelf, on which were kept stocks of tinned and bottled eatables and at one end medicines and dressings. It was a makeshift arrangement, and at times when Bula was in charge, things got rather mixed. Of course, he had never seen a bottle and knew nothing of its contents. His method, when setting the meal-table, was to select the best-looking tins and bottles. On occasion, friar's balsam, vaseline, pain-killer, and boracic acid shared with the butter, jam, pepper, and salt! On one important occasion when the District Officer happened to be dining with 'Nikolo', Bula gave honoured table-space to a large bottle of ink!

One day 'Nikolo' found the youth carefully rolling up an old pair of trousers. He answered his master's query with: 'Alligator's eggs—I'm going to hatch them.' He had found a nest of twenty-four eggs, and had brought two of them home. 'In two days', he said, with face aglow, 'they will be out.' Sure enough, on the second day, two little brutes struggled out of their shells, and began to crawl over the floor. In five or six weeks they had developed enormously, but by this time 'Nikolo' had decided that he didn't really care for such fierce pets.

Bula, the youth, knew nothing of things beyond his own

limited horizon; his island with its strange customs and its superstitions was his world. His friends and relations tried all they knew to dissuade him from attaching himself to the 'misinare'; they played on his fears, they taunted him, they even set the sorcerers to work, threatening him with sickness and death.

But during all this time, Bula and 'Nikolo' were gradually strengthening their friendship. Much time together was spent making preparations for the permanent Mission House. It was a colossal task; a track had to be hewn through the virgin jungle before they could start with their building.

At last the new house was completed, and the glad day came for moving in. This proved a real testing time for Bula. A vicious spirit was said to occupy the particular hill on which they had built—it was a heathen superstition unknown to 'Nikolo'. But Bula knew, and his decision to live there with his missionary friend revealed something of his calibre.

They had not long moved into the new house, when one night Bula came running in with great concern. 'Men are coming up the hill!' he cried.

Together 'Nikolo' and Bula went to the veranda to meet them. They were bringing a grievously wounded man. Angry blood had stirred. There had been inter-tribal fighting. Nor was it all over. With all speed and tenderness, 'Nikolo' set about dressing the man's wounds, removing fragments of bone, putting in stitches. Hardly had he done this, than word came that the fighting had flared up again. At that, 'Nikolo' left the wounded man in Bula's care, and ran to the scene of the quarrel. The poor wretch wounded in battle was the first surgical case Bula had ever seen. It made a great impression. Nothing could drag him from his watch over the sick man. From that moment onwards Bula was always wanting to help 'mend' people.

Mastery of the language also brought the two friends into intimate fellowship. Notebook after notebook was filled with words and midios.

Years slipped by, during which time 'Nikolo' and Bula travelled up and down the whole coast, trying to win the confidence of the people. Ugly gashes were stitched, bones set, and ulcers treated—all without so much as a sign of gratitude.

Then there descended upon the people a reign of terror. The repercussions of this Sito trouble, as it was locally called, had a profound effect upon the work of 'Nikolo' and Bula. Hundreds came to the Mission for protection—every innocent man, woman, and child was made welcome. 'Nikolo' would never forget when, for the first time, the native people expressed concern for his well-being. Now they urged him to keep a loaded gun at his side, to change the position of his bed each night, to lock doors, and cover chinks that might let through the light and betray the whereabouts of his hut. They were the more impressed by this strange man when he confessed that he had no gun, and not so much as a door to his hut. After all, there might be something in the 'misinare's' talk about the protecting care of God. The trader up the coast had fled the island in terror of his life.

And all the time, Bula's heart and life were opening to the Gospel as a flower to the sun. His finer instincts were now dominating his life; one of the early signs had been his desire for cleanliness of body.

When the time came for Bula's baptism, 'Nikolo' asked him if there was any name he would like to choose to add to that of Bula, to symbolize his new life. *'Yes,' he answered, 'I would like to be called Daniel. When my people were so against me, I thought often of Daniel who dared to stand alone, and I wanted to be like him.* When Saul of Tarsus became a Christian,' he added, 'his name was changed to Paul. So mine is changed now, because I am a Christian.'

Daniel became a loved leader among the boys; all manner of things he did with them and for them. Sometimes he would say: 'I am not a white man'—a fact obvious enough—'my father was a black man, my mother was a black woman, and I am black. You will all know that I belong to this place; but although I am not from the land of the white man, I follow the white man's God, because He is the true God.' Then pausing, 'I made a mistake when I said I followed the white man's God. There is only one God, and He is the Father of all peoples of all places. He is my Heavenly Father, the same as He is "Nikolo's" Heavenly Father. . . . You look at me and you see the same face and the same body, but I am new within—my thought is new, my joy is new, my work is new, everything within me is new.'

Daniel's best work, perhaps, was seen in his orphanage. Some called it, with smiles, 'Daniel's den of lions'. There, in a large house of native materials, he gathered waifs and strays from all around.

So sunk in superstition and moral darkness were his people, that even after they began to come to *Lotu*, they came with spears, shields, and battle-axes; no man trusted his neighbour; inter-tribal fighting was still common. As 'Nikolo' saw these fear-ridden people gather, he longed for the day when one of their own would be their preacher. That day came.

Daniel was now a tall, slim young man. He had earned the respect of all. As he rose to speak, the effect of his message was the more striking. As his Master long ago spoke to His country and village, spoke of the seed-sowing and the birds, so Daniel spoke now of canoes, bananas, and shells and storms.

In 1916, after years of work, 'Nikolo' and Daniel and one other came on long furlough to Australia and New Zealand, in order to share the miracle that was happening in their midst. Large audiences gathered. Daniel would sometimes say, 'My master "Nikolo" was angry with me once for having too many lamps burning in one room. He told us we were wasting precious oil. So, I say to you that you have too many ministers and too many churches in one village; you are wasting the precious light of the Gospel. I do not say "Give up using your ministers", what I say is, "Send more of them to the dark places . . ." One thing more—I may not look into your faces again. Let us meet together in the Kingdom of God. There we will not be called white men and black men. We will all be children of the Great Father.'

Daniel's 'Christlikeness' was the most eloquent sermon he ever preached. And he preached the same sermon at home! One Government officer who had received help from him, confessed, 'Daniel, I think, was quite the most refined and best-mannered native I met in the Solomon Islands Group. Please thank him again on my behalf.'

When Daniel married, his wife, Rini, shared his ever-widening service.

∽   ∽   ∽

Then one day word went out—out beyond the homes of his own island people, to the Christian people of Australia and New Zealand, 'The people of Vella Lavella are crying because they will see no more the face of dear Daniel Bula'. His wife wrote: 'My Dani was ill for two days only and then God took him from me. I cannot understand why. . . . But his face at the time of his going was lit with a wondrous light.'

So he passed, Mr. Valiant-for-Truth—*the first dark Christian of Vella Lavella.* One thought instantly of the spirit of that other Mr. Valiant-for-Truth of whom Bunyan told: 'I am going to my Father's; and though with great difficulty I am got me hither, yet now I do not repent me of all the trouble I have been at to arrive where I am. My sword I give to him that shall succeed me in my pilgrimage, and my courage and skill to him that can get it. My marks and scars I carry with me, to be a witness for me that I have fought His battles who now will be my rewarder. And many accompanied him down to the riverside.

'*So he passed over, and all the trumpets sounded for him on the other side!*'

Sixteen short years earlier that young missionary had landed on the beach, built his strange little hut, and ministered to a little native boy with sore eyes.

Forty-nine

'*Blessed be Printers' Ink!*'

'WHEN will the books be ready?' The one eager question was on everybody's lips.

The *Duff* had long since departed, and the little group that she had set down on the shores of savage Tahiti were busy at work. They found themselves amongst a people of whose spoken language they knew not a word; a people who, so far, did not even possess a written language.

It was a lonely life, with no means of escape should their lives be in danger; the nearest white people with whom they could have fellowship, thousands of miles away.

It almost seemed that they must give in, after twelve long years of danger and struggle. Then the dawn came!

No one would ever forget the day when Mr. Ellis and his fellow-missionaries spoke of giving to the people a copy of Luke's Gospel in their own language—*the first copy of the Gospels to see the light of day in the Pacific!*

The eagerness of the brown people of Tahiti knew no bounds. Daily the question was, 'When will the books be ready?' As the missionary and his helpers wrestled with the difficulties of which the people guessed but little, they wondered just what answer to give. The toil of translation over, there remained the difficulty of the imperfect printing-press, with many parts missing or damaged. Happily, Mr. Ellis was no new hand at printing and binding. Soon he had set up his press. The building which housed it was floored with stones dug from the ruins of a heathen temple! It was a token of the dawn, that the very stones which had been stained by human sacrifices, should be put to this new use! Every day brought developments; curious eyes hardly left the printing-house from dawn till dusk. Even King Pomare was anxious to have a hand in producing the first sheets. His people had waited so long! *It was a thrilling adventure of the dawn!*

Materials for the little books were scarce; substitutes for the stiff boards for the covers had to be made from native cloth, several folds thick. The women accepted this task as their share, and sat under the shade of the trees, beating and beating at the cloth as best they could. The men undertook the difficult search for leather. One afternoon, looking up from his work, Mr. Ellis said to one of his friends bent at his work beside him, 'It looks as if all the animals are being hunted solely for their skins. Our printing-office yard looks more like a tan-yard, with its goat-skins, dog-skins—and cat-skins!'

At first, the little books were so precious that many could possess them only by committing them to memory; whole families might be seen poring over one book; some who had mastered the difficult art of writing, managed to copy out the contents on the bark of the paper-mulberry tree.

The precious little books were distributed free, at first; then a plan was made by which the people could make an offering towards their cost. They had no money; they came to the printing-house with bamboo-canes full of oil. The demand at times was far greater than the supply. It was slow work. The sight of as many as thirty canoes lying off-shore was common enough; canoes arrived from great distances, bearing letters laboriously written on plantain leaves, begging a share of the books.

One evening as Mr. Ellis, tired out, was closing the printing-house, five men arrived in a canoe. They uttered the one magic word: 'Luka!'

But there were no copies left. Reopening the printing-house, Mr. Ellis assured them that he would have copies ready for them by morning.

As he looked out early, great was his surprise to see the five men lying asleep near the printing-house, covered with scantily plaited leaves.

'Why didn't you go to the house of some friend, and spend the night comfortably?'

'No,' answered their spokesman, 'our minds would not have been at rest. We would have been afraid lest others should come and take our share of the little books.'

Fifty

'The Seed . . .'

THE four youths stood in the clearing in the bush. A little distance in, stood a small heathen village. Its chief—and the subject of their talk—was a fierce, ill-tempered old Maori. He had shown his temper of late over some kauri logs taken from the bush. The youths had already visited him, and received no welcome.

'We must go again,' said the second youth.

'But he's got muskets and balls,' returned the third. 'The priest gave them to him and taught him how to use them.'

The fourth quoted his New Testament: 'Fear not them which kill the body.'

The ill fame of Kaitoke (Worm-eater) was widespread. Now he had fallen under the influence of this wily native priest who had given him muskets, and had so impressed his power upon Kaitoke as to make the arrogant claim that the death-dealing muskets could never harm him; as priest and friend, he had some secret power against them. Kaitoke had never before handled a musket; his weapons until now had been the simple weapons of his ancestors. True, he had looked fearsome enough, with his lips, chin, and cheeks curiously carved with the greenish-blue lines of the tattoo. But his temper was even more to be dreaded now—who knew where he would stop?

The youths in the clearing turned over these things together. They were not afraid.

All four—Patene, Matiu, Rihimona, and Hohepa Otane—had been among those who had listened to the missionaries. It seemed it could hardly be true now that once they had been afraid of the spirits of their ancestors—the wind in the trees, the rustle of the raupo reeds at the water's edge. A strange new courage had taken hold of them with their new faith. It was 'good news', and they were all eagerness to take it to the village in the clearing.

True, Kaitoke had gone so far as to threaten to shoot them, should they come again. Was he not a man with muskets? Let them hear his word and keep away. There was nothing like a musket to strike fear into the hearts of one's fellows. Crafty old Kaitoke felt that he had handled the matter well.

The four youths were concerned only with a command of another kind; had not their Master commissioned His disciples to take the 'good news' to all people?

Before the sun had gone down upon the hills they had made up their minds.

❧　❧　❧

Hours passed. Then away up the river the missionaries were startled by a messenger. Launching a canoe, they pulled off with all speed, to find the little band of Christian Maoris in a great state, awaiting their counsel. It appeared, from what they could piece together of the dis-jointed story, that the four Christian boys had gone to the village, and true to his threats, old Kaitoke had fired upon them.

One of their number, Matiu, was said to have lived only long enough to say a strange thing, that as a Christian he hoped no revenge would be taken for his death. Rihimona, his friend, had been so badly wounded that his death was just a matter of hours. Patene had somehow escaped, but with three bullets through his blanket. In the midst of the danger, he had courageously stayed to watch over his two companions, whilst Otane, uninjured, had run with all speed, carrying the sad news back to the village whence they had come.

One question now on everybody's lips was, what should be done next? Some were for one thing, some for another. The

N

missionaries, Turner, Whiteley, and Buller could hear that they were not all of one mind.

'*Utu* is sweet,' said one.

'No,' answered another, 'now that we are Christian, it must be different.'

Another interjected, 'But if these go unpunished it will only make others bad. Kaitoke and his people must be punished. If not, we shall never be left in peace.'

Meanwhile, the lad Rihimona died, praying for his enemies.

Night came, and still no decision had been reached. The talk went on; the missionaries crept away to get a few hours' sleep on the floor of the chapel.

Next morning, people were seen to be coming from every direction. Maori couriers had gone out. By ten o'clock, six hundred people had gathered. All the important chiefs had come. Again there was much talk; again it seemed, as on the previous night, that a conclusion would never be reached.

Suddenly, a new factor entered into the discussion; the missionaries offered to go, in company, to the village to reason with Kaitoke and his people.

'No,' said one group after another, 'that would never do. We know Kaitoke, and now that he has muskets he would only kill you, too.'

What should be done? Silence followed—and in the silence musket-shots rang out. Instant fear seized all hearts; many in the crowd imagined that some of their friends had gone to reconnoitre, and had been shot. Many rushed towards Kaitoke's village.

Soon, consternation reigned, balls flew thick and fast; a Christian chief fell mortally wounded. The missionaries who had followed to try to restrain the fear-ridden people, were driven back by the fury of the charge. One after another fell, until ten had been killed. Prisoners were taken, amongst them, the old chief Kaitoke himself.

However, gleams of Christian spirit began to show through.

After overpowering their enemies in the trench, not another blow had been struck; instead of the ancient custom of enslaving their prisoners, they had liberated them, and brought their wounded, including old Kaitoke, down to the Mission House for treatment. To the old heathen chief, this was strange indeed. Still stranger things were to follow.

As the news spread, families from far and near assembled, bringing belongings, that with the missionaries they might be safe. It was a strangely picturesque sight; mothers and fathers with their children; tiny ones too small to walk, tied on the backs of their mothers; older ones, a little shyly, clinging to their mothers' skirts.

For days they stayed. When Sunday came round at last, they gathered for worship; the church, of course, was too small to hold them all, and most had to sit on the grass outside and learn what they could of the service within. At the end of *such* a week, all hearts were strangely stirred. Worship ended, they held a solemn meeting to appoint another leader in the place of Matiu (Matthew) who had given his life.

Busy days and weeks followed. The people began to disperse. Kaitoke had never before received such kindness as at the Mission Station. He had been full of fury and rebellion at first; only gradually had that disappeared.

∙ϴ ∙ϴ ∙ϴ

It was the greatest day the people could remember in the history of the Mission when old Kaitoke himself expressed a desire to become Christian. Each passed on the news to his incredulous neighbour.

Nearly two years later, the people filled the church to overflowing once more. It was not fear that filled all hearts this time. Old Kaitoke was present for the first time at Christian worship.

Would any forget that hush when, after the sermon, the youth Patene stood up to pray for the forgiveness of God for

N*

his would-be murderer? Those present recalled how their Master had prayed for His enemies.

In a very little time the heathen priest who had furnished Kaitoke with the death-dealing muskets, had also made his confession of Christian faith.

The four brave Christian youths who stood that day long ago in the clearing, came to be remembered among the illustrious ones, and no wonder. In every age 'the blood of the martyrs is the seed of the Church'.

Acknowledgements

LOYALTY LIVES STILL. For confirmation of the facts, and permission to use the same, I am indebted to Miss Violet M. Sullivan, Sydney, of the South Sea Evangelical Mission. p. 12.

THE ONE-EYED GOD-MAKER. For his permission to retell this experience I am indebted to Rev. John F. Goldie, pioneer Methodist missionary to the Solomon Islands. Mr. Goldie also checked my manuscript. p. 15.

The Solomon Islands comprise ten large islands and innumerable smaller ones—one of the first important groups in the Pacific known to Europeans. Mendana, their discoverer, it is said, 'named them the Isles of Solomon, to the end that the Spaniards, supposing them to be those isles whence Solomon fetched gold to adorn the temple at Jerusalem, might be the more desirous to go and inhabit the same.'

THE BROWN MADONNA. I owe my thanks to the late James Cowan for his permission to retell this story. During the whole of his long life he moved freely amongst the Maori people, and for fifty-five of those years worked with a magic pen. I am grateful also to Messrs. A. H. & A. W. Reed, Wellington, publishers of *Tales of the Maori Bush*. p. 18.

ONE MORE FLAME! Retold here from *If I Open My Door*— Epworth Press, London. p. 22.

THE OLD PILOT HANDS OVER. Rev. John F. Goldie related to me this experience, and kindly allowed me to use facts from his contribution to *A Century in the Pacific*, edited by James Colwell, F.R.Hist.Soc. Mr. Goldie checked my manuscript. He landed in the Solomons on May 23, 1902. p. 24.

'AS THE GENERATIONS PASS!' For permission to retell these experiences I am indebted to Sister Nicholls, to Misses Shelagh and Inez Fitness, the young teachers, and to Mrs. Mohi, daughter of old Kauia. Sister Nicholls kindly checked my manuscript. p. 26.

The following clipping from the *New Zealand Herald* is of interest: 'A chief of the Ngatimahana tribe, Kauia Tapuke, of Whakaaratamaiti

Pa, died this morning. A prominent figure throughout South Auckland, Tapuke was reputedly 112 years of age. Tapuke's sister who died in 1921 was 103. A *tangi* will be held at Whakaaratamaiti Pa. Among the chief's many descendants is the present Maori King.

'GREATER LOVE . . .' For these incidents I am indebted to Rev. C. T. J. Luxton, late of Skotolan, Buka, Mandated Territory of New Guinea. Mr. Luxton also checked my manuscript. p. 29.

UNTO THE MOUNTAIN TOPS! For help and confirmation of the facts I owe a debt to the *Children's Newspaper* and its late editor, Mr. Arthur Mee, and to *Heroes in Friendship*, by Basil Mathews, M.A.— Oxford University Press. Date of the incident, 1824. p. 33.

THREE MEN ON A RAFT. For their permission to make a digest of *The Raft*, I am indebted to Messrs. George G. Harrap & Co., London, also to the author, Mr. Robert Trumbull. I owe my thanks also to Mr. C. R. Lankshear, L.M.S., New Zealand. p. 36.

'JERICHO ROAD.' For her permission to retell this story I am grateful to Sister Anna Kirkwood, youth editor of *The Outlook*, Presbyterian Church of New Zealand. p. 47.

AN EYE FOR A LIFE. For help given I owe my thanks to Rev. P. Addison Devis, Bolton, England, and for confirmation of the facts, to Dr. Hugh Thomson Kerr's *Worship Story Sermons*—Fleming H. Revell Co., New York. p. 49.

'ONE OF THE LITTLE SHIPS.' For sharing the facts of this experience I am indebted to Sister Lina Jones, also for use of her account of the same as compiled from the diaries of her fellow voyagers. Sisters Lina Jones and Effie Harkness kindly checked my manuscript. The *Fauro Chief* left Roviana, 26 January—arrived Mackay, Australia, 11 February, 1942. p. 51.

THE GOD IN THE BASKET. Sister Ethel McMillan's twenty-five years' diaries, now in my possession, furnished me with the facts of this incident. Sister Ethel McMillan kindly checked my manuscript. p. 56.

'SIGN OF THE NUMBER ONE MAN!' I owe my thanks to the Rev. J. W. Burton, M.A., General Secretary Methodist Overseas Missions, Sydney, for the facts of this story, and for his permission to retell the same. Mr. Burton also checked my manuscript. p. 59.

'FROM HEART TO HEART.' For help with this story I have to thank the British & Foreign Bible Society. Facts were confirmed by

Bishop John Selwyn, a memoir by F. D. How; Isbister & Company, London. p. 61.

Archdeacon and Mrs. Brown lived at 'The Elms', the Mission House, Tauranga.

Ripahau was taken north to the Bay of Islands in 1839, and though a slave, was allowed by his owners to attend mission classes where he learned to read. After the events of this story he lived at Otaki, established as a teacher.

'DREAMERS OF DREAMS.' The granddaughter of Thomas Adams, G. Elsie Harrison, B.A., author of *Methodist Good Companions*, Epworth Press, kindly furnished me with the details of this story. Thomas Adams entered college in the year 1845. The Tongan (or Friendly) Islands consist of three main groups, Tongatabu, Haapai and Vau Vau. About 200 small islands, most of which are uninhabited, are included in the kingdom, covering 250 miles. p. 65.

'ABOVE ALL!' For his help I owe my thanks to the late Rev. R. B. Gosnell, also to two staff members of Station I.Z.B., Wellington. p. 72.

'MAORILAND'S JOHN THE BAPTIST.' The first sermon in New Zealand was preached by Rev. Samuel Marsden at the Bay of Islands, Christmas Day, 1814. Ruatara died in March 1815. For confirmation of certain facts I am indebted to *A Dictionary of New Zealand Biography*, G. H. Scholefield, O.B.E., D.Sc.—New Zealand Department of Internal Affairs. p. 74.

'SHALL HE NOT HEAR?' Rev. Ernest J. Edwards from Malua Theological College, Western Samoa, related to me this experience. With his permission I have recast some of the phrases as being more effective in written form. p. 78.

THE GREAT HOURS STRIKE. I am grateful to the Rev. E. W. Hames, M.A., Principal of Trinity College, Auckland, New Zealand, for access to an old paper, the *New Zealand Methodist*—24 January, 1891, for an article by the Rev. Samuel Ironside himself. Date of incident, 1842. p. 81.

SON OF THE WILDS. I owe my thanks to the late Arthur Mee, editor of *Arthur Mee's Thousand Heroes*, also to the present editor, Mr. Hugo Tyerman, for his kind permission to use certain material. p. 84.

'FOR THOSE IN PERIL . . .' For their permission to use copyright material, I am indebted to Messrs. E. P. Dutton & Co., Inc., New York; for extra material to The American Bible Society, New York; for photographs to the Managing Editor of *The Christian*

Advocate, Chicago; to Schoonmaker, also to the Rev. John E. Barclay, New Jersey. p. 87.

FAITH AND A HANDFUL OF FISH-HOOKS! Record of this historic event is found in *Centenary Sketches of New Zealand Methodism*, by my late Chaplain and friend, the Rev. W. J. Williams. p. 93.

'SURSUM CORDA!' I am grateful to the Rev. J. F. Goldie for the outline of this story. Mr. Goldie also checked the manuscript. p. 97.

'NOT BY THEIR SIZE.' Help and confirmation of the facts were furnished me by the staff of the Presbyterian Missions Office, New Zealand; The British & Foreign Bible Society, and *John Geddie— Hero of the New Hebrides*, by the Rev. Prof. James W. Falconer, D.D., Toronto. p. 99.

'WARRIOR BROWN.' The Rev. G. I. Laurenson, General Superintendent of Methodist Home & Maori Missions, New Zealand, supplied me with the outline of this story. Owing to peculiar local difficulties, The Salvation Army later discontinued organized work among the Maoris, leaving it to the longer established Missions. p. 104.

'ONE OF OUR PLANES IS MISSING.' When war conditions brought Mrs. Emily Sprott, M.B.E., to New Zealand, she shared this incident, and kindly gave me her permission to retell it. p. 106

THE TRANSFORMED ISLE. Confirmation of the facts are to be found in *A Book of* The Bounty—*being Captain Bligh's own record —A voyage to the South Seas . . . including an Account of the Mutiny*, published in 1792; also in *Pitcairn—the Island, the People and the Pastor*, by the late Rev. Thos. Boyles Murray, M.A., F.S.A.—revised and brought up to date by the Rev. C. C. Elcum, M.A., of the S.P.C.K. p. 108.

'WHERE MEN MAKE AN END OF HATING.' For her permission to retell this experience I am indebted to Mrs. Will Stuart, Dar-es-Salam, Tanganyika, East Africa; also to The New Zealand Shipping Company Ltd. (Incorporated in New Zealand), London, private publishers of *Caught by a Nazi Raider*, by Barley, 1941. p. 113.

'YOUNG, STRONG AND FREE.' Miss Inez Hames, for twenty-five years a Christian educationist in Fiji, related to me this incident. It was my pleasure to meet Isikeli when he visited New Zealand with fellow scouts. p. 120.

GOD'S CANDLESTICKS. I am grateful to Miss S. C. Matthews, Church Hill, Kaitaia, New Zealand, and to her brother, Mr. L. J.

Matthews for their permission to retell this incident; also to Messrs. A. H. & A. W. Reed, Wellington, publishers of *Matthews of Kaitaia*. p. 123.

'THE OLD VIOLIN.' The Rev. G. E. Hale, B.A., South Australia, kindly allowed me to retell this experience in a somewhat abbreviated form. I owe my thanks also to the Editor of *The Australian Christian World*. p. 127.

'HIS WONDERS TO PERFORM.' To Mr. Fletcher Wallis, nephew of the late Dr. George Brown, I owe my thanks. Confirmation of many points I found in *George Brown, D.D*—Autobiography—a narrative of Dr. George Brown's forty-eight years' residence and travel in Samoa, New Britain, New Ireland, New Guinea and the Solomon Islands, Hodder & Stoughton. Mr. Fletcher Wallis kindly checked my manuscript. p. 131.

PACIFIC RAIDERS! The Rev. G. H. Eastman, L.M.S., Gilbert Islands, furnished me with the facts, and also checked my finished manuscript. The Secretary of the L.M.S., London Headquarters also checked the manuscript. p. 139.

'THAT DAY!' For his help I am grateful to the Rev. H. J. Odell, Assistant Superintendent of Methodist Home & Maori Missions, New Zealand. Confirmation of the facts I found in *Bishop John Selwyn*—A memoir by F. D. How; Isbister & Company, London, 1900. p. 142.

THE BROWN COMPANION. The Revs. Clarence Luxton, late of Buka, Mandated Territory of New Guinea, and A. H. Voyce, late of Kihili, Buin, supplied me with the facts of this story, and kindly checked my manuscript. p. 143.

'IN DANGERS OFT.' The background of this story I owe to the late Rev. C. O. Lelean, O.B.E. I am grateful to his widow, Mrs. C. O. Lelean of Victoria, for permission to retell it. p. 147.

'THE EVERLASTING MERCY.' I am indebted to Mrs. W. Walker of Auckland, daughter of Mrs. Jory—over ninety years of age—who told the story; and to her friend, Mrs. McHugh of Suva, who kindly checked its accuracy. p. 152.

THE TRAITOR RETURNS. For his permission to retell this story I must thank the Rev. G. H. Eastman, L.M.S. of the Gilbert Islands, also the Secretary of the London Office of the L.M.S. Both checked my manuscript. p. 154.

LOVE TRAVELS SWIFTLY. Confirmation of the facts of this story I found in *Stevensoniana*, by J. A. Hammerton; John Grant, Edinburgh, 1907, and in *The Life of Robert Louis Stevenson*, by Graham Balfour, Vol II, Methuen & Co. Some months before the death of R.L.S., 'at the corner of the road there was erected a notice prepared by the chiefs, bearing their names, which read: "The Road of the Loving Heart. Remembering the great love of his highness, Tusitala, and his loving care when we were in prison and sore distressed, we have prepared him an enduring present, this road which we have dug to last for ever."' p. 157.

'THEN CAME THE DAWN!' *James Calvert*, or *From Dark to Dawn in Fiji*, by R. Vernon, 1890, enabled me to check this historic story. I owe my thanks also to the Rev. J. W. Burton, M.A., author of *Fiji of To-day*. The Methodist Mission was founded in Fiji in 1835. R. W. Robson, F.R.G.S. says: 'The task of civilizing this race seemed hopeless, yet within forty years of the adoption of Christianity by Thakombau, Fiji was tranquil and civilized. . . . This marvellous change was due mostly to the missionaries . . . partly to the high intelligence and adaptability of the Fijians themselves.' p. 159.

JUNGLE TREK! This personal experience was related to me by Mrs. A. H. Voyce, late of Kihili, Buin, Mandated Territory of New Guinea. Ukag—pronounced Ukang—has been supported from the start by my own Sunday School. Mrs. Voyce kindly checked my manuscript. p. 163.

'THE BROTHERS.' I owe my thanks to the General Secretary of the Diocese of Melanesia, Sydney; to the Secretary of the New Zealand Board of Missions; also to the Society for the Propagation of the Gospel in Foreign Parts. p. 165.

DAWN ATTACK! I am grateful to the Rev. G. H. Eastman, and to the Head Office of the London Missionary Society, for help with this story. Both kindly checked my manuscript. p. 166.

'ONE INCREASING PURPOSE.' Rev. Belshazzar Gina, first Solomon Islander ordained a minister of the Methodist Church, related his early experiences to me whilst in New Zealand. For confirmation of the same, and the additional material, I am indebted to the Rev. A. H. Voyce, C.F., who kindly checked my manuscript, and added, 'I heard of the Gizo incident whilst in New Zealand; Sister Merle Farland, M.B.E., corroborated it as I went through New Caledonia; Silas Lezutuni did the same on Vella Lavella; I used it frequently in speaking to the troops. No native ever contradicted it.' p. 172.

'LOVE EVER GIVES!' Mrs. J. F. Goldie, Melbourne, pioneer missionary to the Solomon Islands, shared this experience whilst in New Zealand, and kindly checked my accuracy in retelling it. p. 178.

'THE BROWN DISCIPLE.' For his help I am grateful to Mr. Flewellen King; also to the publishers of *Yesterday, To-day and For Ever*, by William Canton; Hodder & Stoughton, for confirmation of the facts. p. 182.

'AND ALL THE TRUMPETS SOUNDED ... !' To the pioneer Methodist missionary, Vella Lavella, Rev. R. C. Nicholson, author of *The Son of a Savage*, Epworth Press, I owe a debt for his permission to retell these early experiences. It was my joy to meet Daniel Bula whilst he was in New Zealand. For the photograph of Daniel Bula (medalled in London in 1922) I am indebted to Mr. Frank J. Denton, Wanganui, New Zealand. p. 183.

'BLESSED BE PRINTERS' INK!' Confirmation of the facts I was able to find in a book, long out of print: *The Bible in the Pacific*, by Rev. A. W. Murray, 1888; James Nisbet & Co. p. 189.

'THE SEED ...' Patene built for himself a canoe which he called by a Maori name meaning 'Call up the Church!' and went long distances in it, preaching. A descendant, the Rev. Piripi Rakena, furnished me with these facts, per Mr. Flewellen King. Two old books confirmed other facts of the story: *Forty Years in New Zealand*, J. Buller, 1878, and *The Pioneer Missionary—Life of Nathanial Turner*, by his son, the Rev. J. G. Turner, 1872. p. 192.

For help affecting several stories I must thank Mr. R. W. Robson, F.R.G.S., Sydney, the Compiler and Editor of *The Pacific Islands Year Book*.

I owe a debt to the Rev. G. I. Laurenson, General Superintendent of Methodist Home and Maori Missions, New Zealand, for checking the Maori stories.

Illustrations

The dust cover and frontispiece—Lyons.

MAORI GREETS PAKEHA. P. Newcomb. Reproduced by kind permission of Wilson & Horton Ltd., *New Zealand Herald and Weekly News*.

THE HANDING OVER OF THE BOOKS. New York *Daily News*. By kind permission of the American Bible Society, New York.

JOHNNY BARTEK's NEW TESTAMENT. Schoonmaker. By kind permission of the Rev. John E. Barclay, New Jersey and to T. Otto Nall of *The Christian Advocate*.

DANIEL BULA. By kind permission of Frank J. Denton, Wanganui, New Zealand, who took the photograph.

PRINTED IN GREAT BRITAIN
BY WESTERN PRINTING SERVICES LTD. BRISTOL